FROM THE SHIRES TO THE SPIRES

Growing Up Under The Shadow of War

FROM THE SHIRES TO THE SPIRES

Growing Up Under The Shadow of War

by Mildred Masheder

THE WYCHWOOD PRESS

First published in 2011 by
The Wychwood Press
an imprint of Jon Carpenter Publishing
Alder House, Market Street, Charlbury, Oxfordshire OX7 3PH

ISBN 978 1 902279 44 2

Printed in England by CPI Antony Rowe

Dedication

To my wonderful family who have given me so much support: father, mother, brother, daughters, grandson and granddaughter as well as first, second and third cousins.

Acknowledgements

My heartfelt thanks to Judith Rowley for typing and editing, and to Chris Langdon for editing, overseeing the photographic content and helping bring this book to its conclusion.

Contents

List of illustrations

Cover photo: Set Fair for France.

Introduction

From Village Life to the Wider World, 1922-1928

My first autobiography, *Carrier's Cart to Oxford: Growing up in the 1930's in the Oxfordshire village of Elsfield*, is an account of my first eleven years. The village was my entire life: home, farm, school outings with an occasional trip to Oxford in the carrier's cart, our only means of transport.

Now my horizons were gradually being extended: first to Milham Ford School at Oxford, then to teacher training college in London, Paris at the Sorbonne, and finally to my goal of the University of Oxford. Ever since I had been old enough to look down on the spires of the city from the heights of Elsfield Hill, I had a determination to go to this magical place of "castles in the air."

The magic was tempered by the threat of war, which hung over my college days like a black cloud until it became a reality for five long years.

Growing up was a source of exploration of the emotions, intensified by the external forces of war and peace, and finally leading to a settled family life.

At every stage in my travels I always returned to the village in Oxfordshire for my vacations: to Elsfield, then Chislehampton, and finally Ibstone, which is literally on the border line between Oxfordshire and Buckinghamshire. In fact the division was through the scullery! It was always a homecoming and to return to the farm was a respite in the troubled times ahead. Yet in spite of the threat and the reality of war, I found this time highly stimulating as it was a mixture of anxiety, excitement and challenge.

Chapter 1

A New Life at the Grammar School
1927–1935

A new era began for me when I went to the grammar school, Milham Ford in Oxford. It was a complete break with all my previous playmates amongst the village children who had instantly labeled me as 'stuck up.'

Another farmer's daughter, Emily Watts, cycled with me the endless four miles to Oxford in all weathers. At least going was exhilarating, as we whizzed down Elsfield Hill with such élan that we didn't need to pedal until we reached the Washbrook half a mile further on. Coming back was another matter; the long trek homewards culminating in pushing our reluctant bikes in a zigzag motion up the hill, which seemed like a mountain.

I was just eleven years old and the journey to Oxford by bike could be taken in my stride; I had frequently peddled to the centre of the city to the Children's Department of the Public Library. My aim was to supplement the meagre selection of classics we had at home and which I had read over and over again. I knew all my books such as 'Alice in Wonderland' and 'Through the Looking Glass' more or less by heart, and they remain in my memory until this day, ninety-four years later. Every time I went to the library, I immediately made my way to the schoolgirls' section and wallowed in the novels of Angel Brazil.

They were a complete contrast to the boys' adventure stories which mother had read every night to Monty and me and which I had grown to appreciate. It

Monty back from school.

had to be boy's stories; girls had to learn to be flexible. We had our separate comics: 'School Friend' for me and the equivalent for Monty with 'Bessie' and 'Billy Bunter' respectively as the butts of humour. Later, I progressed to adventure stories like those of the French Foreign Legion: 'Beau Geste' and 'Beau Ideal.' Then came the detective novels of Edgar Wallace and the popular 'Raffles.' I became an avid reader of anything that came my way.

It was only at the age of sixteen that I was able to go to the cinema; that was after my family moved to Chislehampton from Elsfield in 1933, and there was a seven o'clock bus home. Then I became an addict of Hollywood films and adored Bill Powell, Myrna Loy, Bette Davis, and a host of others.

On my first day at Milham Ford, it wasn't the dangerous crossing of Cowley Road and Iffley Road traffic at the Oxford Plain that scared me; it was the immense throng of about three hundred girls going into the Assembly Hut. We looked identical with our white blouses and stiffly pleated navy blue gymslips, black stockings and boots. I already had developed a dread of the Headmistress, Miss McCabe, who seemed to be spying on us everywhere at once in her motorised wheel chair. She was badly crippled with arthritis, but that did not make her less severe towards any little schoolgirl, like me, who might literally cross her path. She always wore a masculine-style, gray costume with black boots aggressively planted apart as if to help steer her machine.

How the first morning at school went is a complete blank, except that I recall I was disappointed about being placed in the lowest class, Form 2. This was because I had done badly at the interview in arithmetic. Although I was an expert in the long division of money and questions like how to divide a half-crown by three, or how long would it take to fill the bath if the water flows at a certain rate, the paper for the test seemed to be full of full-stops. I had assumed that they must refer to decimals which I hadn't learnt – only vulgar fractions – so I decided to ignore all the questions with dots. (The entrance interview with Miss McCabe had finished me off.) After discarding my rather blank offering in the way of maths with disdain, she had asked my mother: "*What is wrong with her legs?*" Mother replied: "*That's her combs.*" Sure enough to my total embarrassment my woolen combinations underneath my stockings looked like heavy bandages going half way up my calves. In spite of my fervent prayers, the floor did not open up below me and I was left rooted to the spot in the full glare of her obvious disapproval. So as a result of that interview, I approached the new school with a dread feeling of apprehension.

My parents decided that I should go to my grandparents who lived in the nearby Cowley Road for the midday meal for the first two days. This was a

Miss McCabe.

mistake as friendships would already start to form at lunch-time, but they did it for the best. In fact I don't recall any other decision of theirs to limit my freedom. They seemed always to respect my own judgment, an attitude they pursued throughout my life, for which I am eternally grateful. Unfortunately, that first day, when getting my hat and blazer from the cloakroom, I was caught talking by the formidable maths teacher in charge; I was unaware that it was forbidden. She bore down on me from her immense height, the powerful lens in her glasses focused like mirrors on my bewildered face. *"Go and stand over there!"* she thundered. I did, until the last girl had gone. When I arrived late, my grandfather said jokingly, *"Did they keep you in?"* which I hotly denied.

After this unpromising beginning I settled down happily with two girls, Joan Gibbons and Hilda Haynes from other villages. We were a close trio, always together in breaks and lunch-time. As we were always the top three in the end of term exams, we were all entered for Oxford City's 'Twelve-Plus' Examination. We spent hours exchanging miscellaneous bits of information that we thought might be in the General Knowledge paper such as *"What is the name of the prime minister?"* We all passed; my parents would no longer have to pay the £1 17s 6d per term. This was in spite of my abysmal performance in French whereby I drew pictures instead of composing a sentence in response to *"Qu'est que c'est qu'un chien?"* French later became my speciality but there were no early signs of this.

So the first happy year was passing, but towards the end of a long hot summer, my good fortune suddenly changed. I was going to sit as usual on the grass under the shade of the acacia tree when I saw my two friends already established in a different spot and another girl, Brenda Henman, was sitting with them. I started to join them but all three moved off. I readily joined in the game and chased them. It only dawned on me after some fruitless pursuit, that this was not a game; it was for real. I was dumbfounded. I didn't want to be seen to be all alone so I approached a girl called Dorothy Hughes and asked her if she would like a holiday on the farm. She jumped at it but even to this day I feel an unreasonable anger towards anyone with the name of Henman, even if he was at one time, England's great hope in the tennis championships!

That summer also heralded my first initiation into womanhood: a long-term outlook which filled me with dismay and resentment. The morning after Dorothy arrived to stay I woke up in a state of great anxiety running to my mother exclaiming, *"Mam, there's blood coming out of my bum!"* She was quite casual replying *"That's natural, every woman has that."* *"But when will it stop?"* *"It lasts about five days."* *"And it won't come again?"* *"Oh yes, every month."* I couldn't believe my ears. *"Every month – what – for the rest of my life?"* *"No, it stops when you're a few years over fifty."* That was eternity! I was then given a large square of toweling and an equally large safety pin.

Somehow the inherited legacy of shame permeated my whole being and I went to hide in the only unoccupied room in the house, the parlour, and hid myself on the sofa. The most deadly blow of all was when my mother discovered me, with the words, *"Dad says you are making a fuss."* So he knew all about it. From that day my very close relationship with my father took a new turn; I realised that he was a man and I a woman and somehow a certain reticence had to be maintained. This did not diminish my deep love for him, which remained constant during the rest of my life. He was truly my guardian angel. I only began to appreciate my mother and the great care she bestowed on me at a later date. She had been a victim of 'Spanish flu' at my birth, so I bonded with my father, who had looked after me when I was a baby – as I described in 'Carrier's Cart to Oxford.'

I do not blame my mother for the stark reality she confronted me with, unprepared as I was, and doubtless she had experienced the same unexpected

My mother and her sister, Aunt Glad.

shock that I did. But that was the pattern: not to refer to what was designated as 'down there.' At my thirteenth birthday I could never have appreciated that this particular mechanism would finally reward me with the greatest gift of my life – my two daughters.

My spirits soon rose and I was happy to introduce Dorothy to the delights of living on a farm, especially the harvesting and pony rides. Perched precariously on the slats surrounding the empty wagons we would take bumpy rides down to the cornfields where they loaded the sheaves that had dried in stooks. These were just like miniature houses and we were not too old to play in them and eat the ripe grains, rolling the ears in our hands. Rides on my fat pony, Dot, were equally bumpy; we took it in turns to ride round the field. Dot, who was almost as broad as she was high, was coaxed into a canter with great difficulty and then she was quite likely to stop dead if she spied a dainty morsel to eat. This could easily send us right over her head while she looked on nonchalantly munching.

After a week at Dorothy's home in Headington, I was eager to face the future. Dorothy's father was fascinated with my country talk and went into peels of laughter when I replied to a question as to what I thought of the Pitt Rivers Museum. I replied *"Not so dusty"* – an unintentional comment on the state of the prehistoric skeletons. For my part I discovered the delights of town life. My gastronomic discovery was Marmite!

Next term, in a new class there were new friends. To me the most important thing in life was to have good friends. This time I struck lucky – Jean Graves-Morris, and Margaret Lane – we called her "Bug," and Phyllis Smith, nicknamed "Grub," and Joan Kempster – who we'd named "Fleabite." Insect nicknames were popular amongst friends: Phyllis had asked what grub we should take on a picnic; Joan was always pestering; Margaret didn't like creepy crawlies, but I was always Millie. All four remained steadfast until they left at sixteen and I stayed on alone for the sixth form.

I threw myself into the lessons with enthusiasm. I liked best the English lessons when we acted scenes from Shakespeare. Once when I was Antonio in 'The Merchant of Venice' and Joan Gibbons, who had so abandoned me in my first year, was Bassanio, I had an overwhelming feeling of love for her as I pronounced *"Give me your hand Bassanio – grieve not…. Fare you well… Say how I loved you, speak me fair in death.."*

In History too we acted out scenes which left an indelible mark, like the difference between trial by jury and trial by ordeal and the signing of the Magna Carta by King John at Runnymede. This initiation into the origins of democracy stood me in good stead later on with my interest in politics. My fascination for History led me to be the only girl who scored ninety nine out of a hundred in one exam. The missing mark was due to a blind spot on the counter-revolution. I have written about my passion for Geography and the Geography teacher later.

Art was a sheer delight under the auspices of Miss Fry who looked like a real artist wearing a hand-woven smock. She had a twin sister, Miss Marjorie Fry; they were alike as two peas. She would play music to inspire us and I thought I was painting a masterpiece with an 18th Century couple engaged in a stately dance to the tune of a Mozart minuet. I took it home to finish with great pride, but my mother lent over my shoulder and said *"You've spoilt it"* as I was filling in a very dark green background. I never finished it. Miss Fry also got us to do 'mind pictures.' We had to close our eyes and paint whatever we saw. Mine was a contortion of red veins against a really black background, but she appreciated it! She always encouraged us and that encouragement saw me through into my 90's for I still love painting.

As for hockey I was only once a 'reserve' for the form team, but no one fell out, so I was relegated to handing round the orange slices at half-time, which made me feel inferior compared to the robust players. I did not excel greatly in gym and sports, but I held my own and was never left suspended at the bottom of the rope for ages as was my friend, Bug – when she had no hope of climbing up.

Miss Lamb, the Gym teacher, always looked trim in her rather short brown gym tunic to distinguish herself from our dark blue ones. Her crowning glory was 'The March' on Sports Day when to the tune of 'Colonel Bogie' we set off one by one round the sports field and finally ended up all together in a single straight line. She was always in utter despair at our uneven lines and ranted at us until the day before and then we were suddenly perfect. Later, we learnt rude words sung by the soldiers of the ubiquitous 'Colonel Bogie' and we took delight in mouthing them as we marched. Eventually she came into a legacy and off came the gym slip and she was away round the world on a cruise, and, I hope, romance.

I have written elsewhere in 'Carrier's Cart to Oxford' of my disaster on the one time I was in the cricket team, when after being heralded as an ace bowler (underarm) of googlies, I managed to bowl six highly vertical balls in one over! After that I was taken off, never to return.

Of Miss Fontaine's cookery lessons I have little recall. There were only two incidents, both concerning my refusal to eat what I had cooked. I knew what was in it! There was the occasion when the huge chunks of undercooked cod (the cheapest fish then) were milkily transparent with little red veins running through them. I was told to sit there until I had eaten it, but time was on my side and she had to let me go because she couldn't leave me behind when the crocodile had to cross the conurbation of the Plain in order to return to after-noon school. Yet another time I was made to sit over the stodgiest, lumpiest suet pudding that I myself had concocted, until I had eaten it. Fortunately I spied a chip of turquoise enamel that had penetrated the mess and produced it as my trump card. It was not the atrocious cuisine that Miss Fontaine was trying to punish me for, but the fact that I would not eat what was to her, wholesome food!

I took the two languages, French and Latin in my stride right from the start, but it was only in the sixth form that I began to appreciate them fully. It then struck me that French could be the key to my ever-present desire to explore further afield. So I managed to find a French correspondent through my enthusiastic French teacher and this arrangement would augur a big change in my life.

Latin provided no such opportunities and it was a chore especially when ploughing thorough the militaristics of Caesar's Gallic Wars. However it redeemed itself through Virgil and Ovid, although 'The Metamorphoses' was kept from our innocent minds. I had reached the conclusion that Latin might be left as a more mature choice for those who delight in the derivation of language rather than a compulsory subject at the age of twelve. But it was later in my teaching life that I realized that any aspect of life can be fascinating if taught with complete enthusiasm. One exceptional Latin lesson I shall never forget: Pliny the Younger's eye-witness account of the eruption of Vesuvius destroying Pompei. If I were teaching it today I would have ventured to dramatise it with actual spoken words. Languages are never really dead.

Least popular with me was Scripture under the dreaded Miss McCabe, which did nothing for my spiritual development. We always had to learn three verses from the Bible for homework before her lesson. I was word-perfect the night before with my parents but floundered badly when she quickly surmised that she had a ready victim in her power. The worse part of these lessons, which were always the period before school dinner, was that out of sheer anxiety, my tummy would not stop rumbling however much I tried to suppress it.

I have left until last Arithmetic, Algebra, Geometry, also Science and Botany – we didn't study Chemistry or Biology – was this because it was a girls' school? The Maths, I sailed through but although I worked out logarithms, equations and geometric riders with ease, I could not see any point in them. I could never apply them to my everyday life and interests. With Science I loved experiments: for example, with bunsen burners and little silver balls embedded in wax, proving how heat is conveyed. As ever I had to relate the study to my reality. In the same way I could not work out how to identify flowers from a School Flora, being thwarted at the very beginning by having to decide between monocotyledon and dicotyledon. If only I had been told they were either peas or beans which would always be in pairs, or not (I believe that is the main dichotomy)! But I didn't ask advice; I always knew the names of the wild flowers they produced and worked it out backwards. For our School Certificate (later known as Matric) it was meadowsweet which I knew flourished in soaked, riverside fields.

All of my studies contributed to my burgeoning interest in what education was all about, and my memories show a predilection for active participation in finding out about the world and a creative approach to all learning. I was fortunate to have enough of this mixture to carry me through a largely academic curriculum and to enjoy my schooling.

I would like to pay tribute to all of my dedicated teachers. They were the generation that missed out on family life as so many men had been killed

Mother and father preparing the vegetable patch.

during the First World War. I sensed their devotion to their work and to my education. So many people have been fortunate to have had a teacher who made a big difference in their lives and I had a number of them. They make the big difference to all pupils.

I have concentrated here on life at the grammar school during my teenage years as home routine continued as usual and as is described in my first autobiography.

Evenings were now taken up with homework, music practice, a slice of bread and dripping and bed. The music practice was done more reluctantly as I moved up the school and as I had a change of teacher from the gentle Miss Wiblin – not unlike a gentle character out of *'Cranford'* – to the strident Miss Ball. Everything about Miss Ball was loud, especially her habit of thumping away at my set pieces one octave above my feeble efforts! It was only when she left off while she answered a knock on the door that I realized how puny my renderings of Mozart were.

But then I was a teenager – although we never used that expression. My sights were becoming more and more fixed on the fascination of the big city.

On the lawn with pet rabbit.

So life in the village became dull except when I would gallop my pony through our fields, but the exhilaration was beginning to be tinged with a feeling of loneliness. I found myself more drawn to our new wireless where Henry Hall would relay a passionate mixture of jazz songs: what would be called 'pop' today. I still recall the words for instance, *"I'll never say never again, again, 'cos here I am in love again…to the same sweet you!"* It was the stirring of my heart.

Chapter 2

Stirrings of the Heart, 1932–1935

I was innocent regarding boys until the fifth form when I was sixteen. In the village, in my experience, there had always been complete segregation; the boys went their way and the girls theirs. No doubt the village girls became more experienced than me as my grammar school was single-sexed and there, it seemed that our heart beats were sublimated into 'crushes.' Certainly my emotions towards my own sex ran deep, postponing the time when they would be channeled instinctively towards the boys.

I plunged myself into this mode of having crushes with unequalled fervour. At first it was directed towards ginger-haired idols. As, not surprisingly, none of the staff were endowed with this asset, I concentrated on older girls of prefect standing. One was called R. Smith – I never knew her first name; I just gazed in admiration at her brilliant head of orange hair as she sat confidently at the head of our dinner table and responded to the register.

Then there was Florence Mitchell in the same class. She was more auburn than ginger but that was alright by me. I just wanted to know all about her. I was even so obsessed that I managed to get hold of her diary from her desk to read of her adventurous life. She spent her holidays with her family in a remote part of Ireland having celebrations after probably a dull term-time with a maiden aunt. As I imagined, all the excitement was relegated to the parties they enjoyed by the sea at Connemara with countless cousins. It was such a contrast to my lonely life on the new farm in Chislehampton.

My passion reached a climax one day after prayers when we had quarreled and she wouldn't speak to me. As we were going from Assembly, crocodile-form to the main building, I staged a dramatic faint! It was quite realistic and Miss Overend, the Botany teacher in charge, diagnosed it as 'growing pains' or 'curvature of the spine,' which I suppose could have been true. She took over and escorted me to the rest-room. I calmed down and Florence and I remained good friends – I think she was duly impressed and perhaps flattered.

But this was merely a build-up to my next and final adoration: Miss Johnson, the Geography teacher, Johnny to us girls, whom I worshipped from afar. Although she was neither auburn nor ginger she had the firm lips of my favourite film star, John Holt. She told us to watch the film 'The Trail of '98,' about the Gold Rush. This gave a realistic picture of the desperate plight of the prospectors who had been victims of 'the slump,' and had made one last bid for riches, only to become destitute after undergoing untold hardships. As early as 1934 she predicted that Danzig on the Polish border would be the site of the start of the next war. I sensed and shared her view of the futility of war and this conviction has remained with me ever since, as has my adherence to pacifism. At the beginning of the Second World War in September 1939 as the Germans attacked Danzig, I remembered her prescient words. It was her influence which set me on the path of awareness of the problems of the rest of the world: the huge gap between the rich and the poor and the iniquities of war. But back in my schooldays it was a question of looking up to a model and worshipping everything she said.

The most vivid memory I have of Johnny is an outing she organised to the Chilterns, a beautiful area of chalk hills and bright green beeches, where my family was destined to move to during the Second World War, and where I am destined to be buried. But that day was redolent with the joys of youth as we walked up and down dale singing lustily *'Keep the home fires burning'* – a heritage of the First World War which was still a presence in our daily lives. I felt a surge of happiness just in belonging; I wasn't used to that kind of comradeship and it was often lonely cycling back to the village from school and at weekends without the village playmates who had abandoned me. Johnny's initiative probably inspired me to reach out and to organise friends to share things with, and that impetus has never left me.

But finally the sexual urge was creeping up and the sublimation through crushes came to an end. It probably filled a gap which is relatively unknown today when the sexual drive starts earlier, together with more opportunities to meet the opposite sex and for younger children to aspire to grow up as soon as possible. I don't count a few earlier encounters with a farmer's son in the woods near Stadhampton, when after an inexperienced kiss or two I really wondered if that might have given me a baby!

Our own opportunities were miniscule: the highlight being the joint church service at St Mary's in the High Street when we could eye the boys whilst singing *'Praise my Soul the King of Heaven.'* Otherwise there was the boys' school next to ours, separated only by a fence alongside our playing field and the path to the extension classroom huts. We were honour-bound to have no contact with the boys through the generous slits in the fence. I only recall one infamous incident of forbidden contact: that was when Diana Date (aptly named) was caught passing a letter through the fence to, presumably, a boyfriend. She was expelled! I met her some years afterwards in Oxford and she had an unlikely explanation about it all being a terrible mistake; that she had just picked up a piece of paper that had blown over the fence!

But by the age of sixteen (no less!) the sweet shop at the bus stop outside the school took on the site for romantic encounters. It was owned by Mr. Dance (do people become in some way like their names?). He was old by any standard with a bristling yet drooping moustache. He stood behind the counter in his voluminous apron, smiling benevolently at the young hopefuls who crowded his shop in order to meet the opposite sex.

Once when I was alone in the shop leaning over, intent on sherbet suckers and liquorice allsorts, he suddenly swooped down on me, not unlike a bird of prey, and clasping his arms around me, landed the wettest, whiskery kiss on my astounded mouth. Until then I was completely unaware of his predilection for schoolgirls. The incident did not trouble me too much; I had already suffered legitimately similar wet brushes with drooping moustaches from my Uncles. This didn't stop me from waiting for my country bus inside the shop, but I always took great care to avoid the counter.

My great friend was Joyce Blencowe. I became enamoured of her lifestyle that was centred on making oneself attractive, which, before the age of sixteen, had never occurred to me (really!). For example, she showed me how to make my lips bow-shaped with careful application of face powder and moisture. She was able to get through an acceptable minimum of school work, unlike me and my bosom pal, Margaret, who vied with each other for being top of the class. My sights turned more and more towards Joyce and I cruelly dropped Margaret – just as Hilda and Joan had discarded me. How fickle our friendships can be at that age – we had been so close. Margaret finally told her troubles to our form teacher, Miss Thomson, affectionately known as 'Tommy'. When she summoned me to ask what was going on, I could only try to explain how exciting life was with Joyce and how she had persuaded me to join the Guides on Friday nights and how I could go to tea at her house beforehand and eat *'boughten'* cupcakes and then sleep over at my Granny's. After Guides we would walk backwards and forwards from her house to my Granny's (until I finally realised that she would be worried). Walking together in the brightly-lit streets of Oxford seemed to me to be the height of sophistication – an aspiration towards the high-lights which has never left me. Oxford had always attracted me like a magnet ever since I had gazed down at it from Elsfield hill and this was the beginning of a new adventurous life in the city. All this I poured out to Tommy. In fact Joyce was opening up a vision of a new life of exciting experiences. She had an enormous influence on me;

in fact she was my mentor during the whole of my adolescence. I was the country bumpkin and she was the sophisticated townie.

Joyce and I had now become inseparable after we had been camping together with the Guides in a beautiful Somerset site on the cliffs. The experience of hungrily trying to cook breakfast on a bonfire in the rain did much to bond our friendship.

Besides Guides we always made our way to Mr. Dance's sweetshop after school where we acquired two boy-friends, Basil and Matt, their surnames are lost in oblivion. As a foursome we would explore the beauties of Oxford near the river Thames, like Long Bridges, a wild life area with a swimming area fenced off and where Oxfordshire's renowned fritillaries grew in profusion; not that we were especially concerned with rare wild flowers at that time. I was completely unused to the company of boys and was very self-conscious. I recall sharing my sandwiches (thoughtfully prepared by my hard-working mother) with them and was gratified when Joyce reported later that the boys thought I was a sport. I soon adored Basil; he was handsome with great dark eyes. I sang to myself, *"Basil, my darling, don't you fade away, 'cos Millie loves those dark brown-eyes"* after a then popular song. He once cycled out to Chislehampton past our farmhouse, Marylands, but apparently was too shy to call; he thought that the farm was a cut above his lowly terraced house in Cowley! We drifted apart and I heard later that he was killed in the war.

My next little escapade was equally innocuous: a friendship struck up on the school bus with a sixth-former from Thame Grammar School. He was an ardent rugby player and the zenith of his ambition seemed to get me to go to Thame on a cold Saturday afternoon to watch him play. I resisted. After a number of visits to the Electric Cinema and coffee with large round chocolate biscuits wrapped in purple and black silver paper, we always managed to catch the seven o'clock bus, the last one, back home. Apart from some 'canoodling' at the back of the cinema and in the back of the bus, there was no 'play.' He probably concentrated on playing rugby!

It was still a shock however when at the end of the autumn term, on the early morning bus he presented me with a letter and a packet. The packet turned out to be an elegant perfume, but the letter was calling it all off with no explanation. I was devastated and poured out my grief to my father, who took me in his arms and said, *"You know, it seems terrible now, but one day you'll look back on it and it will have passed."* I never forgot that comfort. My deep feelings towards my father formed an even stronger bond. He had his own troubles after we moved from our beloved Elsfield to a remote farmhouse, a mile from the remote hamlet of Chislehampton. The move from the vibrant

*Mother, father, Aunt Glad,
Uncle Jim at Marylands farm.*

village community life
of Elsfield to the lone
farmhouse in the middle
of nowhere set off a
deep depression in my
mother that permeated
the whole family. My
father's decision to
move, which he later
bitterly regretted, was to escape the contagious abortion that was afflicting his
herd of cows and therefore they were not producing milk. He had hoped that
the new pastures would be free of infection, but alas the cows brought it with
them and there was little hope of affording a new herd. How he managed I
don't know – but he did. It was still the time of the Great Depression and
farmers were struggling to manage to sell their milk and wheat and feed their
families. I regret not having been enough comfort to him as he had been to me.
Perhaps I was; he knew I loved him. But my sights were directed more and
more outside the family, as my mother's depression showed no signs of
abating. Chislehampton was no place for an aspiring romantic teenager,
which became more and more clear to me as my boundaries widened.

I must add that one aspect of the move that gave me a real thrill was seeing
myself as a Western cowgirl, as my father on his horse Diana, and I on
Darkie, drove our infected cattle over the fields to this new abode. I was just
beginning to go to see a film on Saturday afternoons and my idol, Jack Holt
featured in 'the Westerns.' I said to Joyce *"He can ride"* implying some sort of
identification with me and Darkie, my pony. She merely commented, *"They
all do."* I was aware of her superior experience.

The real awakening to the yearnings towards love came from a magical
trip up the river Thames for a whole week of complete freedom. Joyce had the
use of her family punt, especially equipped with awnings should it rain. It
didn't; everything was just magic.

We were seventeen and enchanted with every new experience: at night
lying in our sleeping bags on the river bank staring up at the full moon in the
star-lit sky: in the morning persuading our reluctant bunsen burner to cook
bacon and eggs, and above all, listening to soul records on our ancient gramophone. We played Louis Armstrong singing *'Body and Soul'* over and over
again. This song seemed to penetrate my whole body, if not my soul, and it

*Holiday in Bournemouth:
Aunt Glad, Cousin Beryl,
me and a friend.*

still reverberates at the age of ninety four as I sing with fervour, *"My babes and I are lonely, I've lost my one and only. She was my body and soul."*

Towards the end of this wonderful week it was inevitable that we should meet up with two young men paddling an identical punt with awnings. Joyce, as ever, had precedence of choice and made a play for Derek who was tall, dark and handsome. I had Edgar, who was pleasant enough, but possessed none of these attributes, but he was clearly very keen on me – which was gratifying. When I went to London for teacher training I was glad to have a boyfriend.

I have memories at night being wedged together prone under the discreet awning listening to our "soul music," the gramophone perched precariously at our feet. It was the depth of feeling which stirred and reverberated in my heart. Nothing happened except glorious feelings of a thrill that penetrated my whole body. I suppose there was some snogging; it seemed that by mutual agreement this was sufficient.

We had to part the next day in order to reach our destinations; they were heading for London and we were due to be picked up at 3pm that afternoon at Abingdon bridge by my friend Francis Phillips. Actually in spite of frantic paddling we didn't reach the bridge until dark; Francis had given up after four hours of waiting! There had obviously been a lot of dillying and dallying on the last morning as we exchanged addresses with our newly-acquired friends.

On my return to Chislehampton I had plunged further into the father-figure stage. It was Francis who became the next object of my affection.

Francis was the forty year-old owner of the garage and blacksmith's shop at Stadhampton where I took my pony to be shod. To me, Francis was a romantic character with his rich golden hair and eyes as blue as my father's. He was obviously a father-figure plus my predilection for ginger hair! He had somehow run away to Egypt and had lied about his young age of fourteen to join the Air Force in the First World War. We often went swimming together in the Thames. I was keen to have him lie on top of me in my swim-suit, but he declined saying *"people would talk."* I couldn't think why, which shows how innocent I was! Our friendship continued over the years and he was always a support whenever I returned to Chislehampton in between my travels.

Although my interests were increasingly elsewhere, the support of my parents always provided me with a sense of security during those teenage years. I had become very conscious of the way in which my body had filled out, to the extent of being somewhat plump, and had therefore put myself on a strict diet. My mother was affronted by my steadfast refusal of her home-made cakes. Was it a question of mild anorexia? When some affluent visitors, the Landstads, came to buy fresh eggs and brought a huge carton of ice cream in an ice box, I rushed to the granary and weighed myself on the heavy weighing machine; I was down to seven stone and could indulge!

This mood that had suddenly captured my whole being in the fifth form showed no signs of abating in the sixth form. The enchantment of Oxford and the attraction of Joyce Blencowe's company was more pervasive than ever,

Feeding the chickens with two posh visitors from Oxford, the Landstads, who came to buy eggs.

although my absorbing interest was no longer Friday night Guides – but boys.

This was a time of change in my family life as well as the emotions emanating from my own inner self. Life had become lonesome. All of my friends had left Milham Ford after the School Certificate. Margaret was doing a secretarial course; she would have been really welcome now. Grub became a nurse, and the others found jobs serving in the more elite shops of Oxford. Joyce had started training as a chiropodist and looked very professional in her immaculate white coat. I felt overgrown in my gym slip and school hat when I called in.

These changes did not endear me to the uninspiring curriculum of the Higher School Certificate. I didn't see the point any more of working just to pass exams, so after much deliberation I applied for a two-year course in teacher training at Whitelands College in Putney, London.

Chapter 3

Leaving Home, 1935–1937

After the glimpse of romance on moonlit nights on the Thames, reality imposed itself in the form of two reluctant years spent at Whitelands College in Putney training to be a teacher. I felt at a loose end; study had no longer any aim, the way it did for the School Certificate. That's the trouble about working for exams; it can destroy the enthusiasm for study for its own sake. I was still imbued with the strong feeling of rebellion that discarded previous value systems without replacing them with something worthwhile. My reluctance to envisage a mere career in teaching was accentuated by my disappointment in abandoning hopes of being able to go to university. But then I also was not in the mood for study.

My mother was keen on me going to training college and becoming a teacher because she had been a trained teacher and had held an assistant's post at Felsted Training College in North Oxford. The point was that I had no ambition whatsoever to teach. However going to a university was expensive. My childhood vision of going to Oxford now seemed unattainable. My Auntie Mildred happened to be staying at the farm when I had to make the decision about my future career. She had attended Felsted Training College while my mother held a post there as an assistant to a lecturer. Auntie Mildred, apparently had a crush on my mother who was highly flattered and promised to name her first baby girl after her; hence me. Now the roles were reversed; she had become very bossy and my mother was a pawn in her hands. They were adamant in deciding that Whitelands in Putney was the College for me. *Faute de mieux*, I acquiesced. At least it was in the big city. It is strange to think that a lack of direction on my part and also too much direction on theirs, hoisted me into a career which has been my dedication. But the devotion took many years to mature. It took a whole decade and even then I had no choice – I was called up! Meanwhile I made my way to Putney with apprehension. I had never lived away from home and knew I would miss the care that I'm afraid I took for granted.

The College had certain traditions aimed at creating a family atmosphere. Every new student had a godmother (no godfathers!) and groups of five godchildren and their godmothers made up each family of ten who had to sit together at every meal for two years, although of course the composition of the group changed by five every year. That was all right if you got on with your family. Most of mine had rooms together – all with lovely views – including my very own godmother's. However, my room was isolated on a different floor at the back of the building. I have always been very affected by a room with a lovely view and this was the opposite as it looked on to dustbins. I tried hard but not hard enough when the new college friendships were forged. Good relationships, to my mind, are the basis of a fruitful life and somehow I never achieved that at Whitelands.

The restrictions irked me unduly: compulsory chapel (high church) morning and evening, which at least left me with a deep appreciation of the beauty of plainsong. Lectures were equally compulsory with only Wednesday afternoons and weekends free, enabling a permitted escape from this soulless modern building in an isolated area on the way to Putney Heath. Escapees were signed 'out' and 'in' with reasons why; for example, 'theatre visit' or 'home': with details. As the West End theatres ended at ten thirty, it was a marathon to get up West Hill to clock in by eleven. If you were late by minutes, you had to have a watertight excuse. My most convincing one was that I fell off the last bus, which was inaccurate in that in spite of great effort, I didn't really get on the bus, only a piece of my shin remained there as I tried to board it while it was gathering speed. The theatres were worth the trauma: there was Ivor Novello in 'Glamorous Nights,' and the sophisticated Noel Coward in 'Private Lives,' and the riveting musical, 'Anything Goes.' Again, love of theatre has continued to be a passion – also opera which has replaced for me, modern day musicals. It is interesting how pursuits in one's late teens can evolve into lifelong pleasures.

Was it because my commitment to teaching was so lukewarm that I found the daily round uninspiring? The atmosphere was so imbued with restrictions that it was more prescriptive than the grammar school. There were however, some inspiring lecturers who had a great influence on my future approach to teaching.

One was the dynamic English lecturer. She was black – an early arrival from the Caribbean – called Miss King. She was refreshingly outright, calling attention to British reluctance to use such Anglo-Saxon words as 'bum,' much to the embarrassment of some of the rather stuffy trainees! She introduced us to new writers like Willa Cather and inspired us with a love of Homer's 'The Odyssey.' At her first lecture she asked us to write an essay describing ourselves. I gave an unfavourable account of my appearance as I was

College Play: a dramatic performance of the comic ballad, 'John Gilpin'; wearing a mob cap in the front row right-hand-side.

convinced then of the unprepossessing nature of my looks – although, when I look at old photos they belie this. I had written that my eyes were too small and that at my birth, my mother had apparently asked the doctor if they could be enlarged in any way; at least that is what she told me. Miss King sent for me to see for herself, close-up, what on earth I looked like. She made no comment on my looks, but she encouraged me in my writing, which gave me much-needed confidence and sowed the seeds of my future enthusiasm – although it took a long time to bloom.

Act ll of 'John Gilpin'. I was the hind-legs of the pantomime horse!

The other highlight of my studies was my chosen main subject – French. This was a revealing choice as no French was taught in the elementary schooling for which I would qualify to teach. I was voting with my feet against teaching! Languages were then the domain of the selective grammar schools for which a specialist degree was required. My enthusiasm for French was fired by a burning desire to spread my wings and that meant crossing the Channel, and by specializing in French I set my sights resolutely in that direction. My French tutor at Whitelands, Mademoiselle Lagarde, was all that I could wish for: inspirational, witty, unconventional, and above all, she took a personal interest in her band of students. She was a breath of fresh air in the somewhat stifling atmosphere of convention. Later at Oxford I was to admire the outrageous stance of Enid Starkie, an *'avant garde'* don, whose specialities were Verlaine, Baudelaire and Rimbaud. She was the *'enfant terrible,'* stalking about Oxford in slacks and a French beret jauntily perched at a sharp angle. Lagarde, as we affection- ately called her, was of a similar outlook. She enlivened her sessions with little anecdotes of Parisien life. I recall one about Paris under siege in 1870. Was it her great-grandmother who smuggled rabbits (skinned) when she returned from the country, under the eyes of the city's customs authorities? When questioned about contraband, she said *"Cherchez dans mes pantalons, si vous voulez,"* and in fact there it was, in her knickers! When I came to leave, it was Mademoiselle Lagarde who helped me get my scholarship to the Sorbonne and for that I was, and still am, eternally grateful. So, my path was set.

Weekends could be lonely even though Edgar usually took me out on the Sunday. I recall one lonely Saturday that I decided to visit inmates in the 'Home for Incurables' next to the College. The very name sent shivers down my back. At least they would be more unhappy than me – or would they? All of them had been seriously injured in the San Francisco Earthquake of 1903 and had been hospitalised in London ever since. I bought them lots of sticky cream cakes and the atmosphere was very animated. It made me feel a whole lot better which I'm afraid was the point of the exercise.

Another lone expedition was the occasion of the funeral of King George V in 1936. The crowds were tightly packed. As we strained to see the hearse and the soldiers marching to the doleful beat of Chopin's funeral march, an elderly woman next to me said, *"But they ain't for the likes of us."* When I wrote to tell my father he reminded me once more of the dangers of the ever-present White Slave Trade! Another historic event I witnessed was the burning down of the Crystal Palace in 1938. The blaze kept going all night long.

On the Channel ferry to my beloved Paris.

I was already in Paris in spirit and by the Easter vacation of my first year at Whitelands, my plans were all set: Newhaven-Dieppe £2 17s 6d – London to Paris – staying for a fortnight with Paule Flacon, my French exchange correspondent. As her mother had sadly died, shortly after Paule's visit to our farm, the atmosphere was rather sober. I tried conversation on my first evening during the soup course…*"Le plafond est **très-haut?"(trezzo)*** Monseur Flacon pointed an accusatory finger at me and shouted *"**Très haut, très haut, très haut,**"* with not a vestige of liaison between the two words! As Paule was working during the day, I had plenty of time on my hands to explore Paris. Everything was enchanting: the merry-go-rounds in the Luxembourg Gardens, the rose windows of the Notre Dame, the Champs Elysees to the Arc de Triomphe. The weekends were spent with Paule and her boyfriend Jacques, at Versailles and Fontainbleu. When we were alone for a moment Jacques tried to date me! To my shame I agreed and we met secretly. Paule was working on weekdays and he wasn't. I just wanted the company and we went to the Bois de Boulogne where King Edward the Eighth was soon to stay after his abdication. With Paule's approval I allowed him to correct what I fondly called my 'thesis.' It was on the Impressionists, which had always been my passion and still are.

The uninspiring two years in Putney were made bearable by my liaison with Edgar of the punting encounter. No longer the romantic magic of a night under the stars, our relationship wouldn't be called an affair. He was a lifeline for me, this reliable man from Upminster who had a steady but junior job at the 'Pru' (the Prudential Insurance). Our liaison lasted a year and a half while I was at Whitelands. It was a relief to take the tube to the end of the district line to join Edgar and his parents, where the Sunday lunch was an escape from college, and the focal point of the whole weekend. I have to confess that I would buy a ticket to the next station for a few pence, then say I had lost my ticket and pay only for one stop before my destination. Money was in short supply. No wonder they tightened up the restrictions. Alternatively he would take me down to my family on the farm and we would sing '*When I Grow too Old to Dream*' and sea shanties round the piano. What was his attraction? Probably his little Austin Seven that was my escape route from the rather uninspiring college that I felt had leanings towards a nunnery.

Edgar and I spent one summer holiday camping for a fortnight in Scotland travelling in the Baby Austen. It was an endless amount of traveling from London to the Trosssachs, then across to Oban on the West Coast and then all the way back. I couldn't drive and with Edgar, the energy of his sex drive seemed to have been consumed by so much driving. Anyhow the nippy nights kept us both well tucked up in our respective sleeping bags in the tent. The scenery was sublime and our feelings duly sublimated. Would that happen today over seventy years later? I realise how he shouldered all the responsibility for what was a wonderful experience of the beauty of Scotland.

We kept up the relationship until the following Easter, 1937, when at a party I flirted with Edgar's attractive brother, stirring up sibling rivalry. It was unpardonable I know: I blame it on two glasses – or three – of red wine I had drunk, which always affected me. I only danced with the brother; I can't remember Edgar dancing. We parted. Without my escort, I concentrated on my French studies with my sights firmly set on the scholarship to the Sorbonne. Years afterwards I heard he was living in Essex, near the sea, with his wife and two children. He was quoted as protesting against the beaches still not cleared of mines after the war.

The two-year teaching-training course finally dragged itself to a halt and I was back on the farm. Now I was a trained teacher and could get temporary posts in the Oxfordshire village schools – once I could drive there. But Paris was beckoning.

Chapter 4

Romance in Paris, 1937–1938

I am finally coming to the conclusion that we make our own destiny; our purpose becomes manifest as we, often subconsciously, seek out new avenues of experience and make relationships with people who are mutually attracted to ourselves. It was Joyce who arranged my first introduction to Oxford life. By this time, she had many contacts with the university.

One such incident was an invitation to tea. It was at an Oxford College – Merton or All Souls – this detail is now beyond me. It was enough to experience at first-hand a bit of my dream, growing up in the village of Elsfield, which looked down from the hill on the *'city of sprees and spires.'* I could clearly distinguish the spires and I soon found out the meaning of sprees. I yearned to be a part of it and I suppose the tea party was to be my first spree.

I am amazed, looking back, that I had to get my mother's consent. It must have been that Auntie Mildred had come from Liverpool to stay for a week and that we had arranged to go to Oxford on the bus. My mother was dubious – I ought to stay with them, but Auntie Mil won the day with, *"Oh let her go!"* So a young girl of twenty just about to spend a year in Paris had to get clearance for an innocuous tea party – or was it? Perhaps my mother's instinct for safeguarding her offspring was uncanny.

The tea party itself is now surrounded in a mist of romanticized memory. All I recall is that there was a tall, dark and handsome Lebanese man called George Moore and a charming young Frenchman called Marc Janin who turned out to be the nephew of the Prime Minister, Leon Blum! We must have exchanged addresses as they were both going to play a significant role in the next few years of my life.

After the tea I arrived late and apologetic at the humble dairy in George Street where Mother and Auntie Mil were having a snack of welsh rarebit. I was full of the most exotic cakes I'd ever tasted and there was a new sparkle in my eyes. I was determined to go to Oxford! The contrast of cultures was one that would be with me for the rest of my life.

I met George the next week at the Cadena Café in the Cornmarket at Oxford. This was an elegant nineteenth-century-type café boasting its own palm court orchestra (complete with palms) and we sat back, serenaded in comfortable cane chairs over our coffee. To my shame I had the *'culot'* to point out to him how people were staring with hostility at him, but that I wasn't prejudiced; on the contrary I was proud to be seen with him!

I am afraid traces of my inverted prejudice are revealed from time to time. Where did they come from? There were no black people, no Jews, and only one disabled person in my village childhood. This was Perp Newell, the hunchback, who was my brother Monty's constant companion and I certainly felt repulsed by him. Similarly when I was living at the Cité Universitaire in Paris I felt anti-semitic towards Rita Abel, a fellow student who was of a swarthy complexion, very fat and had a decidedly hooked nose. There was also a much older woman student who was constantly on the arm of a young, very disabled, spastic Hungarian student. I'm afraid we students were all united in our disgust of the pair! There didn't seem to be any African or Indian students around so my racial prejudice did not manifest itself. In growing up I must have absorbed all sorts of prejudice without being aware of it.

My first week in Paris turned out to be highly dramatic. The course at the Sorbonne officially started at the beginning of November but I had been too impatient to wait until then and arrived at the Franco-Britannique College a week ahead of time, via my accustomed route, Newhaven/Dieppe £2 17s 6d return, London – Paris. But I was not alone: I traveled with George (we were now firm friends since the tea party), my incipient racism completely overcome as far as he was concerned! Here there was complete freedom – no one knew where I was from or what I was doing – which proved to be only too true!

I just checked in at the Cité Universitaire and left my baggage; did I take an overnight case? I don't recall. Everything was so spontaneous. We sallied forth into a Paris seething with life and activity. It was 1937, the time of the Great Exhibition along the banks of the Seine, the highlight for me being lunch in a restaurant on the deck of a special barge overlooking the Seine bridges in both directions. George recommended sauerkraut which turned out to be not to my, still unacquired, taste for vinegary cabbage. It was whisked away and replaced with gourmet chicken, *Poularde de Bresse,* I imagine, at considerable expense.

What stands out in my memory of the International Exhibition was the contrast between the British and the Soviet Collections: the British concentrated on the hunting equipment of the gentry: hunting pink (actually scarlet) jacket, snow white trousers, long black slim boots and silver stirrups with a crested crop. That was all. I have never been in favour of fox hunting. The Soviet presentation was dominated by a much larger-than-life statue of a radiant, idealized, Soviet couple – both in a striding position with their right arms stretched to the sky, representing the glorious Soviet future, rather than heaven.

Paris was our oyster; we roamed endlessly by day, having coffee at the famous *'Dome'* and *'Les Deux Magots'* cafes in Montparnasse where we hoped to catch a glimpse of Jean Paul Sartre or Simone de Beauvoir. We never did! By night we clambered up the steps to the flood-lit gleaming cupola of the Sacré Coeur. To me it resonated of the exotic Orient. Our favourite haunt in Montmartre became *'Le Lapin Agile'* where we consumed cherries soaked in cherry brandy and listened to the French traditional songs – *'J'aime toujours le chant des cerises'* played on the accordion. We joined in heartily, to the accompaniment of the accordion. This was Picasso's favourite café and his pictures adorned the walls. On our very last evening together, George had no more money. This meant that we couldn't afford *'Le Lapin Agile'* – I slipped him a hundred franc note and said *"Are you sure you haven't any money in your pockets?"* It was still the man's pride to pay and I must admit that I was glad of the tradition as my sparse scholarship money would have been greatly erased in the whirlwind of our extravagances.

Then came reality. After seeing George off back to Oxford I went back to the Cité Universitaire to embrace my new life of study. I happened to arrive at the same time as two 'goody-goody' colleagues from my teacher training College. They looked at me as if they were seeing a ghost! The police had been searching for me; my distraught parents were convinced that I had been kidnapped by the white slave trade, which my father had warned me about. On my previous trips to Paris he had always insisted that I sewed my money inside my corsets just in case. I had complied rather reluctantly, but I couldn't quite see the connection. They would surely find it! My parents had been in touch with my French correspondent, Paule Flacon who soon dismissed my false claim that I had been staying with her. I was immediately summoned to Monsieur Declos, the director of the Franco-Britannique Hostel. I tried to exonerate myself unsuccessfully. He quickly got down to brass tacks; *"What was the address of the young man?"* I innocently asked why? Of course it was obvious but I found it beyond me to be explicit. I wasn't brought up to talk of 'that sort of thing.' I just said that it would be impossible and that was true: as a Middle-Eastern gentleman, George felt he couldn't deflower a virgin! Monsieur Desclos took the address – in case. He was after all, a French man. I kissed him on impulse – I felt he understood.

As I write I realise how thoughtless I had been to cause such anxiety to my parents. I should at least have found out how to buy an airmail letter card or a telegram to say conventionally that I had arrived safely, but in embracing my release from the confines of my training college and my mother's possessiveness, it had never entered my mind.

Chapter 5

Scholarship to the Sorbonne, 1937–1938

After the week of romance, the reality of actually living in Paris was pure magic. It was as if I was being transported to paradise and it did not prove to be disappointing – on the contrary it was everything I could have wished for.

Joyce's influence still held sway. She even came to Paris with two boyfriends, one for me, which dovetailed perfectly between my initial week of abandon with Georges and my more permanent relationship with Yves. My conscience was sorely pricked at cutting so many lectures during my first week at the Sorbonne. I once broke out and impetuously dashed off to attend one lecture and then spent the rest of the day enquiring for them at their hotel: a fact that was not lost on Joyce who reported it rather gleefully when I clocked in dutifully the next day. From then onwards the influence waned; I took over the mantle of what I imagined was the real high life.

But it was Joyce, a few years later after a whole series of boy friends, who finally hit the news headlines as 'Princess Brighteyes!' It was a perfect description. She was blonde with blue-grey eyes which were both languid and sparkling, and her lips were sensuous and her nose "tip-tilted like the petal of a flower." She became something of a celebrity in the press in the romantic tale of the tailor's pretty daughter who had become engaged to a handsome Malayan prince –

Joyce Blencowe pictured in a newspaper.

Tungku Makmud, the brother of the Sultan of Tregganu. They had met while he was studying at a public school in Oxford. He was besotted with her, on one occasion flying to her bedside at the John Radcliffe Hospital after she had fallen ill – he had been on a liner taking him home – he jumped off the ship when it docked in Marseilles. I have the newspaper report.

They were determined to get married despite the Sultan's strong disapproval of his brother marrying a non-Muslim, the newspapers said. Tungku Makmud's car was confiscated and he was cut off without a proverbial penny (I don't know the currency). Unfortunately I had met them by chance in Oxford that very morning and hadn't read the papers and innocently asked them for the £2 they had owed me for some time. Joyce reacted strongly saying *"Give her the money!"* I tried to explain when I found out, but she didn't believe me. For some time we were estranged and the rift took some time to heal, but it did. We renewed the friendship when I was married to Harry. Then we lost touch over a number of years. I heard later that they had split up and that he went home and remarried, so ended a major influence in my emotional development. .

After the excitement of the week with Georges and its consequences I was amazed how soon I settled down to student life. The very idea of living in Paris continued to be a dream. I wanted to be dressed *à la mode* and before I went I had bought some navy-blue material in soft wool. Joyce was fashion-conscious and had made it into an 'above-the-knees two-piece.' I loved it and it gave me a whirling sense of freedom every morning as I jauntily entered the glass doors of the Institut Franco-Britannique, admiring the reflection of my shapely legs – as we had not been accustomed to skirts quite as short.

On my first shopping expedition on arrival at the College, I sallied down to the Porte d'Orleans market to buy the most alluringly fitting, black velvet, two-piece. All that was needed to complete the two outfits was a white lace blouse and every month I bought a new variation on that theme. This was my only extravagance – from a dainty little shop next to Barclays Bank in the Rue du 4 Septembre, where I called for my carefully rationed installment of my scholarship grant.

My room at the College Franco-Britannique, part of the Cité Universitaire, was a perfect dream – everything was perfect! It was decorated in a pale blue woven material with carpet to match, with modern light beech furniture and divan. It was mine! Also the room had a wonderful view of the trees bedecking the Cité Universitaire; *"Quelle est cette agglomeration de Bâtiments?"* asked Felix de Grand Comble – a writer of one of our set books – chosen to initiate us into the wondrous variety of Paris. The Cité Universitaire had its own varied architectural style: the Swiss students were accommodated in a chalet and the British were in a mid-nineteenth Century, imitation Edwardian building. There were always 50% of French students in every hostel so that we would fraternize – and we did.

Each national building had its own breakfast café with hot French croissants and real French coffee. I stared ignorantly at cartons labeled *'Yaourt'* and decided, with my British prejudices, that I wouldn't risk them!

We would all assemble at the International House for meals and we women soon learnt to throw our coats over our shoulders and never use the sleeves, just like all the French women did. Steak and chips was our favourite: the chips had the French touch and so did the steak, although we could have done with much sharper knives.

The chief entertainment was a selection of French films shown in the huge auditorium and they were free. They always began with the three knocks on the floor according to the tradition of the French theatre. These little touches *"à la française"* thrilled me, as did everything French. I sighed over Jean Gabin's firm but sensual lips in *'La Grande Illusion'* and the dashing looks of Yves Menton. The film that stands out in my memory is *'Carnet de Bal'* in which Marie Bell, as a recent young widow, decides to trace all the partners signed for in her first dance programme. This was the custom in her youth. They all turned out to be louche characters – I recall her visit to Louis Jouvet who thinks she is a client for his back-street abortion business. She recites Baudelaire's poem *"Vois-tu toujours mon nom en rêve?"* whereupon he replies with the sardonic, *"Non!"*

Life at the Cité Universitaire, was just one example of the fairy-tale fantasy I wove under the enchantment of Paris. I was relatively unaware of the trouble brewing in Europe except to believe, as all of us did, that war was inevitable. I was very conscious that the French franc had fallen and I knew where in the newspapers to look up its continuing fall. My unaccustomed interest was that the value of my scholarship had trebled and the franc was now the equivalent of a penny, halfpenny which could buy a coffee at the bistro down the road at the Porte d 'Orleans where we sauntered every night after dinner. I learnt afterwards that the fall of the French franc was due to the bitter attacks on the socialist policy of Marc's uncle, Leon Blum, who was Prime Minister. The forces of the Right had contrived to make his policy fail by forcing the devaluation of the franc!

Yes, it was 'we.' How lonely it would have been otherwise. I soon was swept into a close friendship with *'Pheeleese,'* my English best friend; that's how I pronounced her name as we had a pact that we would never speak a word of English to each other, but always practice our French. *'Pheeleese'* had a better grasp of French than me and was fluent, but she had the most appalling French accent, which did not improve as the year went by.

We both acquired boyfriends early on: mine was Yves Camou – half Niçois, half Breton – and hers, André Mercier; they were both medical students. *'Pheeleese'* had a theory about men in general, and Andre in particular, summed up in her excruciating French: *"Il faut qu'ils souffrent, Meeldred, Il faut qu'ils souffrent!"* And he so did! She made a point of always keeping him waiting, which was inconvenient to us all, when we had a foursome.

But she was devotedly true to him and managed to get a job as an assistante in a French Lycée in Normandy after our year was up, so that she and Andre' would be able to be near each other. I never saw her again. The war intervened. She had written to me from Annecy immediately after the war saying that they had a little girl and were so happy and would I visit? But when I finally came to Annecy some years later she was dead. After the war on my way hitch-hiking to Italy with a teacher friend, we stopped off at Annecy hoping to get the promised invitation to stay. I phoned and received the most complicated response in French with a real dose of the subjunctive. Translated it went something like this: *"How can it be possible, that you did not know that she was dead?"* It was probably Andre's mother, landed with the care of a small girl. Did the war cause her *('Pheeleese's')* death because of malnutrition during pregnancy? This was the unoccupied zone where they were often starving, except for the young French girls who accepted a ride in a Nazi lorry.

Back to the contrast of our idyllic days in Paris. Yves and I always went to Les Grandes Boulevards during the weekends. They were ablaze with lights in the streets and in the grand cafes of the Champs Elysees, where we could afford two coffees. I was still rather a country bumpkin and early on distinguished myself by walking into a mirror wall in one of these majestic cafes. I was so impressed thinking that the whole place was twice as big. But our favourite pastime was to frequent the *Boîtes de Nuit* to dance our version of the tango which was more Franco-British than Spanish. The nightclubs were always packed so that we were the equivalent of 'bumper to bumper.' Once when Charles, Yves' friend from Nice, visited Paris we took him to an up-market *boîte* with entertainment consisting of a revue of naked women who all had a basket strapped round their most vulnerable part. The audience was invited to land balls in the net to the pop song *"I'm putting all my eggs in one basket."* My incipient feminism prompted me to walk out in disgust followed very reluctantly by Yves and Charles.

Lectures at the Sorbonne and the British Institute figure less in my memory but they were taken in my stride. I can't say we were wholly devoted students;

suffice that we passed the Sorbonne exams at the end of the year. I only recall one oral exam: on French history. It was quite frightening, conducted in French by an auspicious historian named Monsieur Ceignebos. Fortunately we had studied his publications and so had ready answers. The papers that I really sailed through were those on French literature especially the novels.

It was my study of the novels of Emile Zola that sparked off an interest in the iniquity of the famous or rather infamous Dreyfus affair. I must confess that my complete absorption in Zola's novels was due to their explicitly sexual content rather than his sense of injustice in the *Affaire Dreyfus* manifested in his document '*J'accuse.*' It is worth recording the Dreyfus Affair in some detail as it had a profound effect on my burgeoning socialism and indeed on my incipient anti-racism.

Zola had accused the French establishment, particularly the top brass of the military and the clergy, of deliberately condemning Alfred Dreyfus, a high-ranking officer, of spying for the Germans. Dreyfus was Jewish and German–speaking from Alsace, and France had just suffered a humiliating defeat when Germany had annexed Alsace and Lorraine. In a violently anti-semitic court martial, he was condemned for life to Devil's Island where he was bound hand and foot to his bed with no communication with his warders.

Finally Zola's manifesto, together with Dreyfus' family, secured a retrial but again he was condemned with false evidence, which was not released – for obvious reasons. By this time a fellow officer called Ferdinand Esterhazy had been implicated but was allowed to flee to England to live out his days in Harpenden! So finally Dreyfus had to be pardoned although still condemned as guilty, but by this time he was a broken man unable to communicate.

This disgraceful blot on the political landscape had a great effect on me. It resonated with my intense feelings about justice and played a part in consolidating them. A further connection was that when Marc Janin's Uncle, Leon Blum, was Prime Minister before the war, he linked the pernicious anti-semitism of the Dreyfus Affair with the Nazis. In the same way, his policy of *Le Front Populaire,* which had socialist tendencies, was bitterly attacked also on the basis of anti-semitism. This led the way to the establishment of the Vichy Government during the Nazi' occupation of France; they turned out to be more virulent than the German occupiers in sending Jews to the death camps. For me it was the end of my anti-semitic tendencies.

The year at the Sorbonne was coming to an end all too quickly and I would soon be returning to the confines of Chislehampton, leaving Yves behind in France.

Chapter 6

A Visit to Germany and Poland, 1938

Soon the exhilarating academic year in Paris would be drawing to a close. There was already an atmosphere of *'fin de saison'* in the hot, half-empty streets. *La retraite* was about to begin, when for three months many Parisiens sought the sea or the countryside, and thousands of school children departed for their *'colonies de vacances'*.

My own plans were a reluctant return to the little hamlet of Chislehampton; so how could Yves and I continue to be together? It was goodbye to the Cité and the College Franco-Britannique, our breakfasts and dinner always together; the nightly trek to the Café St Orleans for a prolonged coffee with an occasional treat of *'une coupe de champagne'* (which cost the equivalent of four pence!) and the weekly visit to *'les grandes boulevards.'* We would then saunter back to clock into the Franco-Britannique before one in the morning. As our efforts to study together had not proved fruitful, Yves had not presented himself for his medical exams as he knew only too well what the outcome would be. He called on his imagination to describe to his father in graphic terms the burly examiner with a black beard. His father merely handed him the note he had received from the Medical Board; that his son had not presented himself. So he had to return home to Nice to take all of his exams in the late autumn.

Then the unexpected possibilities of widening my horizons fell into my lap: Nina Plucinska, a fellow student, invited me to stay at her mother's farm in Poland. This was exciting. I managed to get the remains of my scholarship funds out of the bank and planned the long railway journey. I decided on a few days stopover in Berlin with Erich.

I had met Erich Kraus when I was still a schoolgirl. Cycling home after swimming, I overtook a backpacker as he was toiling up the hill. We talked enthusiastically and when I finally got on my bike I quoted romantically Longfellow's poem: *"Ships that pass in the night, and speak to each other in passing...only a look and a voice, then darkness again and a silence."* My thoughts had only recently turned towards the opposite sex and this tall, blue-eyed German had stirred my feelings. There was a twinge of regret that I would

At the lakes outside Berlin.

never see him again. At this stage my emotions could be sublimated in love for my pony, galloping over the fields, though all too small. Imagine my reaction when the next morning, all flushed from the ride, I found Erich sitting at our kitchen table regaling himself with hunks of bread and dripping and hot cocoa – our usual hospitality to travellers and tramps alike. I'm not sure if my parents had ever met a German, except Mr Gatz of Beckley. There was plenty of anti-German feeling after the First World War, but although my family shared the general patriotic approach, there was nothing in their hospitable demeanour that reflected it; to them he was an interesting human being. To me also! We exchanged addresses and he sent me a book of German paintings: one I recall was a picture of young people dancing round a tree at the top of a hill. It seemed quite romantic.

So it transpired that four years later in summer 1938 I initiated an invitation to stay for a few days in Berlin with Erich, now married with a wife and their two young children. I wasn't in tune with children that young: I liked teaching ten year-olds and was horrified to pick up from my scanty German, that they were begging their parents to be able to wake me at six am and the parents equally emphatically insisting on not a minute before half past six!

So half-past six it was and we made friends. They revelled in a picnic expedition to the beautiful lakes and woods on the outskirts of Berlin. We all swam in the icy waters with a stoicism that was worthy of the Women's League for Health and Beauty. I think this was of German or Nazi origin and it had certainly spread widely in Great Britain. Joyce and I had joined it with enthusiasm and called ourselves 'Vim and Vigour!' There was a lot of arm and body swinging to music, all with a radiant smile. I don't think it survived the outbreak of war.

I was not at all politically conscious at that time, only hoping against hope that we would not go to war. I had no idea of the devastating effects of the rule of Hitler in Germany over the previous five years. When I asked Erich about it, he said he had been unemployed under the previous Socialist Weimar Republic and had not been able to feed his family on the inadequate benefit. Now he was a teacher – so for him life under the Nazis was an improvement. He said he would take me round Berlin the next day and to a political gathering so that I would understand the situation better.

Now my memories of Germany grow dim. I only recall walking along the Unter den Linden and having my first taste of *wurst* sandwiches with no butter, on tough rye bread, which were indeed the 'worst' I've ever tasted. The political reception has become even dimmer in my recollections. I am almost too ashamed to write what I recall. All I know is that I was presented to a small dapper-looking man with dark, sleek hair and fiercely penetrating blue eyes. He held out his hand and of course I shook it. Did I realise at that very moment it was Joseph Goebbels, Adolf Hitler's Propaganda Minister – himself? I think I did, but I wouldn't have dared create an international incident by refusing his outstretched hand. But these were *'illusions de grandeur'* probably triggered by recent revelations of Hitler having an alliance with Great Britain through King Edward VIII, later the Duke of Windsor, who was

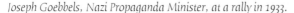

Joseph Goebbels, Nazi Propaganda Minister, at a rally in 1933.

Polish peasant woman gathering the harvest.

a Nazi sympathizer and who visited Hitler, in 1937, after his abdication.

Erich announced to his family how Goebbels had shaken hands with me and we left it at that. He probably sensed my feelings of shame and betrayal. I have kept secret this incident for over seventy years, being ashamed to admit it, especially to my Jewish friends, many of whom were refugees from Hitler's rule. So the next day I was on my way to Poland, taking with me memories of a warm family destined to suffer. As with all my European friends, I would never see them again.

What a contrast from Berlin – the rural tranquillity of the farming land near Poznan in East Poland. Nina's mother, Madame Plucinska, was a widow, toiling on an equal basis with the farm workers. It was the time of the rye harvest which by now was ripe and had to be reaped early starting at half-past two in the morning, otherwise the hot sun

Madame Plucinska working in the fields.

would cause the seeds to fall. I can see her now bolt upright on the mower and then the side rake, just as we did on the farm at home. I felt that close spirit that links farming communities throughout the world.

My attraction though was less on mutual affinities in cultivating the land than on Madame Plucinska's two handsome sons, Wieslaw and Jurand. I appreciated their gallant attentions to me, kissing my hand with a regal flourish. I decided I had fallen in love with both of them; I couldn't choose

On horseback with Jurand and Wieslaw Plucinski.

Jurand Plucinski – my favourite.

between them! I have a photo of the three of us on horseback.

They were noble souls and quite spirited, as were their steeds. It was quite terrifying as I was used to my pony who measured quite a few hands less. However I managed to hide my fears and pass muster with these two officers in the Polish Cavalry. A year later, in September 1938, when Hitler's army invaded Poland, there were widespread media reports that they were ordered to charge against the tanks with disastrous consequences. This was apparently untrue but they performed acts of great horsemanship and bravery as the Germans took over Poland. Wieslaw was killed that September, but Jurand somehow managed to escape, and landed up in Africa from where he contacted me years later after the end of the war. I was by then happily married to Harry.

But back in 1938 it was an idealistic Polish summer – constant blue skies reflected in lakes and rivers. We roamed the meadows and harvested fields and I felt I was back in the Oxfordshire countryside. One activity I could not bring myself to participate in was wild duck shooting which was a favourite sport of Wieslaw and Jurand. I was reminded of William Hazlett's poetic description of the desperate fluttering of the stricken bird before it crashed down to the earth. When we had roast wild duck for supper, that image rose before my eyes and I struggled to appear to be enjoying every morsel.

On Sundays we would drift by boat to the little Catholic church in the nearby village. The rowing boat was just big enough to take five of us, down the slow-flowing river. One day Madame Plucinska took me to see an aristocratic family. I wanted to stay behind with my new-found boyfriends but she said I couldn't disappoint them. I understood why: all the children were what we used to call 'mongoloid.' The house and

Enjoying the Polish countryside.

grounds were stately and the children full of smiling goodwill. I was prone to start thinking of a degenerate aristocracy. I hope I've learnt a bit more since then!

A further example of my brashness was when the time came for me to depart, I only had enough money to get home on the long, third-class train journey. A lavish picnic was packed lovingly for me, including a whole roast chicken. Seeing my plight, Madame Plucinska saved the day by offering to lend me money for the substantial tips for the servants! I did pay it back via the bank and they sent the photos. Their hospitality was like that of my family which I felt and still feel is akin to all those who live on the land.

It was a good homecoming, after a long journey by train, when I made the mistake of changing money for a longed-for cup of tea in Belgium francs and it cost me a pound: an outrageous amount. I

With Patch back home in the garden at Marylands Farm.

didn't always sufficiently appreciate the luxury of having a welcoming family home to retreat to when I returned to Oxfordshire, tired and penniless. There was never any criticism of my absences and the love was always there in abundance.

Chapter 7

Wintering in Nice, 1937–1938

After Paris, Germany and Poland, life seemed dull on the farm at Chislehampton. My pony had died from laminitis (fever of the feet owing to the damp). The fields were often sodden or even flooded in their proximity to the tributary. My feelings of guilt over Paris and the high life were extended to Darkie's swollen hooves and fetlocks as described to me in detail by my brother Monty, when I came back from Poland.

But even without a steed to trot to the next village, Stadhampton, where Francis Phillips still owned the smithy and garage, I could cycle there. He was literally a staple support and gave me driving lessons with saintly patience. I was not brilliant at changing gear up a hill and was haphazard in reversing – a trait which has remained with me to this day, although automatic cars have made gear-changing a feature of the distant past. Our relationship had changed – no longer the calf attraction of a school girl still in a gym slip towards a First World War fighter pilot. We did celebrate his exploits by visiting Hendon Air Display. Francis treated me to a trip in a two-seater bi-plane. What I didn't know was that he had tipped the pilot for some 'extras.' So I found myself looping the loop and staring up at the earth. The cockpit was completely open and I felt very relieved to have a seat belt! Francis had a good laugh.

The change in our relationship was marked by two incidents; the first indication was at Stadhampton Fair on the green. I had bedecked myself in my marina blue (turquoise) two-piece which I had 'run up' myself on mother's hand sewing machine. This now antique machine had apparently been torpedoed during the First World War and its instructions were in Portuguese, possibly an export to Brazil but I soon cottoned on! Marina blue was all the fashion; named after Princess Marina of Greece, who had come to England to marry into the Royal Family.

To my discomfort Francis was already enjoying the bumper cars with a sophisticated-looking woman, his arms around her! We were introduced to each other then off they went on the galloping horses. I soon went home, recalling as I peddled disconsolately back, gossip about Francis being a womaniser. The fact that I had been in Paris for a year with Yves had little bearing on my feelings of rejection!

Francis was not embarrassed by his conduct at the fair saying that she was an old friend. Later we arranged to spend an afternoon at Oxford, Francis driving me in his old 'banger.' Turning out his purse, he asked me to choose whether we hired a punt and went up the river Cherwell to swim or whether we should have a walk along the towpath and then go to Fullers for tea. Although I still had memories of Fuller's coffee layer cake on a previous invitation by the headmaster, brother of Miss Stace, my primary school teacher, I chose punting and a swim.

Refreshed and hungry after the swim, Francis artlessly proposed stopping in for tea with a family he knew. The family consisted of Mr. and Mrs. Barraclough and their ten year-old daughter and a magnificent spread was miraculously already on the table. Did I sense the frisson between Francis and Mrs. Barraclough or was I too intent on cakes to notice? Certainly they were as animated as Mr. Barraclough was subdued.

It was some time later when the penny finally dropped. My father had to settle a bill with Francis and as he passed by his cottage window, there were Francis and Mrs. Barraclough engaged in a passionate embrace, springing apart when they realised they were being overlooked. Francis made some feeble excuse about tripping up on the carpet, but my father came home saying that that was not right with a married woman. It was unforgivable in those days. He might have been swayed in his indignation by my obvious relationship with Francis. Much later I heard that she had got a divorce and married Francis, leaving her then teenage daughter with poor Mr. Barraclough. So ended my attachment to a father-figure with not too much emotional upheaval; we did remain good friends. But all the time I was pining for France and Yves – in that order.

After some negotiations, Yves' parents invited me to stay for the autumn and winter. I was thrilled – the South of France – just like Scott Fitzgerald! I think they realised that this was the only way of insuring Yves' internship at the hospital of Nice was to have me captive under their eyes. Indeed I was well chaperoned. We had bedrooms next door to each other but never entered each other's. I bought them presents: a splendid dressing gown in dark red satin for Monseiur Camou and a hand-embroidered set of tablecloths for Madame. I realised afterwards that the presents were unequal and women don't necessarily appreciate table linen, however fancy. Still, she did not hold that against me. It must have been difficult for her to accept that her only son's affections were lavished on someone from another country and where he might eventually go to live.

Picking oranges with Yves Camou in his family's garden in Nice.

I went to the Education Centre of Nice every day and prepared for my Oxford Entrance, which they would invigilate. Yves went to the hospital each day, and we would assemble for a late midday meal. In the afternoons Yves and I would explore the environment in his father's car (he was Chief Engineer of Nice), or we would take walks along the sea front on the Promenade des Anglais. The evenings did tend to go slowly however, taken up mostly with the dinner ceremony, starting always with soup and meandering towards fruit for desert, which were oranges from the garden. It was a lifestyle however that suited me royally and so began a whole series of visits to the Mediterranean later on in my life.

Yves had been in the habit of taking a coffee with his friend, Charles Gastaud, who lived nearby. When I wanted to join him in a spirit of equality it was pointed out that that would make it a formal occasion with the ladies having to be present, Madam Gastaud and Lucille, the twenty year-old daughter – and with the best coffee set laid out with dainty sweet-meats. I could understand, but chafed at the restrictions imposed on women.

In fact there was a ' La Traviata' scene under my very eyes. Charles had an Italian mistress, who had been more or less a courtesan, and who was now living with her mother. It was made clear to Charles that marriage to Pierrette would somehow spoil Lucille's chances of marriage! So Pierrette was not recognised by the family. Fortunately the declaration of war, when Charles was immediately called up, put an end to this prejudice and they married on his first leave.

Yves' other friend, Nico, was in a similar position, but with a tiny pied-à-terre to entertain his girlfriend Nicole, who was also beyond the pale – as far as his parents were concerned. To me it felt like something out of the last century. Nicole confided in me that on vacating the bed, she placed a few hairs in an identifying pattern to reassure herself when she came next time that Nico had not entertained any other lady in the meantime. I was duly impressed with her ingenuity and thought this was France, keeping up to her reputation of passionate love affairs.

This was brought home to me at Christmas when Yves suddenly became ice-cold towards me. His mood matched the weather as it was the first time in living memory that there had been heavy snowfall in the South of France at Christmas. The Camou family were driving to Marseilles to celebrate Christmas with a solitary grandmother. We only got as far as Toulon as the main road was completely blocked with snow so we had to spend a shivering night in a miserable little hotel. At least it wasn't a stable, which on second thoughts might have been warmer! Certainly Yves' mysterious mood added greatly to the chill.

During a restless night when reluctantly I shared a room with Madame Camou, she enlightened me as to Yves' fury. Apparently Leah the live-in maid had searched in my chest of drawers and found a letter from Marc Janin. He had written in French of course, to ask if I would like to join a skiing party near Grenoble with George and other friends of his. I had been flattered to be remembered and had written to decline and had forgotten all about it. It took a long time to convince Yves of my complete innocence and that making up a skiing party did not imply a sexual attachment. Although I have to admit that the jury was out about what would have happened if I had gone!

Leah was a mournful creature and I believe I invited her envy and I wasn't experienced enough to have been on my guard. Judging by the plaintive songs she sang, I gathered that she had probably been crossed in love. When she sang *"J'attendrai, Le jour et la nuit, j'attendrai toujours,"* it was so convincing that she would wait forever, but to no avail. She was not blessed with any of the attributes that would attract the opposite sex: she had a swarthy complexion and was blessed with a singularly large nose. Probably she had had a difficult life, not least because of the anti-semitism that I was becoming increasingly aware of.

So the wintery Christmas gave way to sunshine and Nice celebrated the Battle of Flowers. I was somewhat ungracious about the front seats in the Promenade des Anglais that had been reserved for Yves and me by his father. I objected to the term and action of the word 'battle.' (Was the threat of war hanging over my unconscious?) To me it seemed that thousands of carnations

were being plucked from their natural life and then used as weapons in a continuum of fights between paraders and spectators until the street was layered high with mountains of dead, mangled flowers. At least I paid tribute (literally) to their beauty by sending my family a huge bamboo container full of every colourful variety. They lasted for weeks.

Although the storm clouds of war were gathering, life in the South of France was one round of pleasure with little thought about what was lurking ahead. One of our favourite haunts among others was Jimmy's Bar up in the hills at Cagnes. There we could have English tea and buttered toast from a sort of eyrie looking down on the magnificent view of the sea below. We often made a foursome, with Charles and Pierrette, picnicking near the sea with Pierrette making her famous *'pain bagné'* – french baguettes soaked in olive oil and stuffed with olives and anchovies *à la niçoise.'* Sometimes we would have a private meal at Jimmy's where we danced through the night. On one occasion they compared the succulent French chicken cooked on the spit with the British culinary tradition. With red wine dashing through my blood, I felt bound to defend our delicious farmhouse chicken tasted only once a year on Easter Sunday. I was quite belligerent about defending my native cuisine.

In somewhat of a haze I do recall dancing several times with Charles which did not greatly please Yves, who reproached me as we drove home. The next day we all got up early to go skiing at Breuil in the Alpes Maritimes.

Pierette, Yves, and myself on the right holding skis.

I was fearless to begin with, Charles' praise of *'les anglaises sportives'* ringing in my ears as I swept down. Alas pride came. I managed to fall so that the upturn of the ski struck my nose and I was indeed a sorry sight.

I then thought it opportune to apologise to Pierrette if I had flirted with Charles the night before. She was sophisticated enough to say there was no question of any such thing. I felt out of my depth, but after that incident little twinges of doubt stayed in my mind about my future together with a jealous husband.

Nevertheless our relationship was now restored to its former equilibrium fanned by the knowledge that we would soon have to part. With our plans for Yves getting a post in London as a doctor at the French Hospital, I was as determined as ever to go up to Oxford. Somehow I never faced up to the implications of being separated not only by fifty miles, but by a completely different culture pattern. There had been other twinges of doubt: was Yves anti-semitic or racist? He had made a couple of anti-semitic remarks about photographs of Jewish friends of mine and there was obvious racism towards the very black Senegalese soldiers stationed in Nice. There was certainly a vast amount of prejudice in France, as indeed in England. But these fleeting thoughts did little to disperse the rosy idyll woven around our lives. It took the stark reality of the impact of the Second World War to seal our destiny once and for all.

Chapter 8

Earning My Way to Oxford 1938–1939

An interview for Oxford awaited me on my return to England! I never doubted that I would have one, nor indeed that I would be accepted. In fact I might have been under the illusion that I was God's gift to Oxford, a conceit that was soon to be knocked out of me. The interview started with the question; *"Were you in a hurry when you wrote your papers?"* Thus began the demoralising process. Should I say yes or no? I had vivid memories of being stumped on the no-choice essay; it was on 'Punctuation.' With hindsight I realised that they really didn't want to know the difference between a semi-colon and a colon, nor the intricacies of the apostrophe – something on the lines of 'eats leaves and shoots' would have been appropriate.

I unfortunately tried to redeem myself by saying, *"My French is good"* (and under my breath); *"it blinking well ought to be!"* Then I received the full blast of the Oxford accent; *"I presume, Miss Clinkard, you mean that your French is up to standard?"* There was an emphasis on the last syllable of my surname, as that of *'standard'* with a prolonged vowel *'a'* sound. I was put in my place.

Were they short of candidates for an 'exhibition'? Whatever the reason I was accepted and all I had to worry about was to supplement funding for the next three years starting October 1939; also how to fund myself until then and make another trip to Nice.

First I had to pass my driving test; supply teaching on a short term was the only avenue open and I was a qualified teacher. That meant I had to be at the disposal of Oxfordshire Education Committee and to be prepared to go to any village school by car. Francis Phillips was the answer to my prayer as he was a driving instructor – and the fair at Stadhampton and even Mrs Barraclough were a memory of the past. I had bought a minute Austin Seven for £4.00, which I named Yvonne. It had a rather dilapidated hood that kept quite a lot of the rain out, but mostly I enjoyed the sense of freedom with the hood down. It was like being in a box and Francis as my instructor had nowhere to put his long legs. After intensive practice I passed the test!

Unfortunately this success went right to my head and as I was in Oxford and the test examiner had made his willing escape, I decided to drive round

Me and my cousin Beryl pushing Yvonne, my Austin Seven, at Marylands Farm.

to all my relatives to tell them my good news. Some years before I had visited them all on my new pony, Darkie. I was always a show off!

After receiving the complements due to me, and Yvonne, I found myself outside the Cowley Road cinema and realised I could see a film and then drive home at my leisure. But the car park was full. When the burly commissionaire saw my little box-like Austin Seven he said *"Come on, we can find room for that little 'un."* I should have known better; he called out *"back, back, back"* and I did – *crunch*! I saw the film, but with no appetite, and was the last one to leave the apparent security of the cinema. I think I was fondly hoping that the matter would just go away. I hadn't even dared look to see if there was any damage.

Two insurance agents greeted me and it then turned out that my last temporary insurance policy had expired that morning. Addresses were exchanged. I gave the address of Watlington School where I was going to teach on Monday, so that my parents would not know. Letter after letter came until I forked out the £5 17s 6d. It seemed a lot. I was lucky not to be fined for driving without insurance and the insurance brokers seemed kind and understanding. They didn't want any hassle.

Alas that was the end of poor Yvonne, my ancient Austin Seven. (She had had fortnightly temporary cover notes from every one of the seven insurance companies in Oxford, always being refused when presented in person as it were.) I was lucky; one of the teachers at Wallington wanted to sell her car for £16. It was a black Morris Saloon and only had ventured to the nearby villages once a month or so. I called it Robin pronounced *à la française*. If only I had kept Yvonne in a barn on the farm she would have become a museum piece.

So began a completely different life of village school teaching, miles away from the luxury of the Riviera. I drove Robin everyday from Chislehampton to Watlington via Charlgrove to pick up Miss Currill and Mr Richards, both teachers at the school. The money for petrol was scrupulously divided into three. When I returned home, tired after a day's teaching, my mother had kept a generous helping of the midday meal between two plates on a saucepan on

Mr. Milnes – my landlord and Quaker mentor.

the range. (It reminded me of the 'tea dinners' at Elsfield when the men returned from the day's shoot and when my brother and I enjoyed a full dinner with them after school.)

I don't think Miss Currill thought much of my powers of discipline; she seemed to take some pleasure in pointing out "*Your class was playing 'merry-come-up'*" – a favourite Oxfordshire phrase. I was able to take the rigid pattern of lessons in my stride as it was identical to my own village school at Elsfield: Assembly, Scripture, 'Mental' Sums, English, History or Geography – and then various arts in the afternoon. The senior girls' needlework was what you might call a teaching challenge; I was seduced into cutting up their dresses round their bodies. Anyhow it seemed to work – that is until the Home Economics Inspector came. He was really dishy and asked me if I was free in the evenings. I reassured him that I was as free as the air, only to discover that he was recommending a basic needlework class at Henley-on-Thames!

One visitor to the school brought great good fortune to me however. This was Mr Milnes, a devout Quaker, Bursar of Wadham College, Oxford who visited schools voluntarily. When he heard of my determination to go up to Oxford, he offered me board and lodging free in his house in Five Mile Drive in North Oxford. I had meanwhile discovered that my future college was somewhat misleading in its title, 'The Society of Oxford Home Students'. This meant you could only live at home if it was in the City of Oxford within five miles of Carfax, not in some remote village like Chislehampton. I jumped at the generous offer. I had been concerned about the expensive item of students' digs – minimum prices were £4 per week! He kept his word. In my eighties I joined the Quakers, the Society of Friends, and have found great friendship and devotion and I recall Mr Milnes with gratitude.

Money was still going to be scarce so I applied to the Oxfordshire County Council for a loan over three years; no grants were available. I had to face a stern body of hard-headed men. The maximum amount was apparently £15 per year, but even that had to be fought for. *"What would you do if you were unable to pay the loan?"* was a 'googly' bowled at me. Somehow dazzled by the intense attention this seemed to arouse, I said boldly *"My father would sell his cow."* This seemed to satisfy them and the great deal was struck and I felt my roots in the farmyard! I did pay up.

So the summer term at Watlington County School came to an end and I said goodbye to the headmaster, Mr Slaymaker (who had a famous bull-nosed Morris open car, just like Miss Staces' at Elsfield School). Goodbye also to Miss Currill and Mr Richards, who would both be biking to school next term when I would be at Oxford.

A job soon fell into my lap at the Examination School Board, in the High Street. It dealt with entering the marks for School and Higher School Certificate, which fortunately needed no mathematical ability on my part. My cousin Basil had managed to recommend me and as money to get to Nice to join Yves was my priority, I jumped at the opportunity.

Whilst entering rows of figures into a ledger, my thoughts were far away on the Riviera, savouring the crystal blue waters of the Mediterranean. An idea struck me. If I could get ten people to have a holiday in Nice, I could get my return fare paid and have enough over to buy clothes for the Oxford winter. Again I never linked the plans for Oxford with my still passionate love for Yves; or was it more a passion for France and everything French?

There was an agency in St. Giles that catered for everything, including holiday groups. The owner took a personal interest in my project and was as keen as I was to get the ten people. He persuaded his divorced wife and two children to go. Later I fully sympathized with him in getting a divorce. By recruiting a few colleagues from the Examination Board, we finally made up the numbers. The bargain was ten days in the South of France – £10.00, every-thing included – travel and accommodation. It really was a good deal – at least it could have been. The accommodation was four star with all meals provided on the terrace. The hotel was perched right on the sea with a glorious terrace on stilts very near the famous Promenade des Anglais. I should have wondered why it was empty at the end of August 1939. I won't dwell on comforting nine people during the stormy passage from Newhaven to Dieppe – at least, I thought I won't be coming back with this lot and this was only too true. How on earth did I get them from the Gare St. Lazare to the Gare de Lyons with a demanding meal in between? I just remember sinking exhausted into my hard, third-class seat for the night. By morning the sunshine of the Midi revived us and as soon as I finally got them all settled in the hotel, I escaped to be with Yves and his family.

My feelings in retrospect were that there was only one real drawback to this bargain of a holiday and that was the date: the ten days encompassed the fatal September 3rd, 1939 with the declaration of war with Germany.

The divorc*ée* with two children felt that it was my fault that the war broke out; she had been even more unaware of the political situation than I had been. I suppose we had been living in an ignorant fools' paradise – there had been that scare the September the year before with Chamberlain, returning from visiting Herr Hitler in Munich, coming back with the spurious message, *"peace in our time."* The group all gradually departed in dribs and drabs before the actual declaration of war. Before they went, we took one delightful couple, to the monastery garden of the famous piece of music of the same name. I found some peace of mind there high up above the sea, surrounded by flowers. The 'peace in our time' which had been promised a year ago was gone forever.

On the night of my arrival, Madam Camou had arranged a charming celebration of our *'fiancailles'* with an elaborate gateau and Yves presented me with a diamond ring. On September 3rd, Yves tuned in to London and we listened in stony silence to the message that we were at war with Germany. That night Yves was on medical duty at a night-club in Monte Carlo. We danced to the plaintive song of *"Tonight I cannot think of you, Music Maestro please."* The tears were pouring down my face as we danced our last tango together. In a few days Yves received his call-up papers to report to a base on the ill-fated Maginot Line. Charles and his friend had already been summoned to the *Alpes Maritimes* (memories of carefree skiing). He left in a state of exhilaration that I could not share. This seemed part of the unrealistic optimism, compounded by the oft-repeated, *"Oh les aura, quand même?"* (We'll get them, whatever happens).

We set off a day earlier so that we could make a clandestine stopover night in Marseilles, the only time we had been able to stay at a hotel as a couple during the whole time in the South of France. Barriers were already beginning to break down because of the war. Charles was at last able to marry his Pierrette.

I didn't sleep. All night long we heard the intransigent sound of soldiers marching to war. My anxious heart beat in unison with their implacable steps. We still had some hours left on the train before we parted at Lyons, forever as it turned out. But as we made our way through the crowded compartments, who should greet us but Yves' aunt, as sophisticated as ever! I could feel her eyes on my dishevelled appearance indicating that she knew what we had been up to. Did we have our last precious moments together? Memory draws a blank, but I am pretty sure that we found seats elsewhere; we were past caring what got back to the Camou family.

All I recall is standing bereft, alone and solitary in Lyons station – the sounds of Yves' train getting dimmer in the distance. Everywhere was pitch-black – France had taken the blackout very seriously. No trains to Paris until tomorrow morning. I clutched my heavy suitcase and made my hesitant way towards where I thought the centre might be. I was not to know that the station was perched high up and great flights of steps led to the town. After falling down the first flight I groped my way to the first available hotel – a squalid affair.

Somehow I staggered back home and the nightmare journey was finally over. I was once more in the care of my loving family. In Britain it didn't seem as if there was a war on; everything was eerily normal. Soon children were going back home after the immediate evacuation as there had been only one alert – to test the sirens. What amazed me was the interest in cricket matches, both locally in Stadhampton, and nationally. This reminds me of the famous film *'The Orient Express,'* when the two 'Brits' didn't have a clue about the murder; they were just devastated to miss the test match! In that case, *'Rain stopped play,'* when they arrived at Victoria, much to their relief. At this time, it was a case of *'Phony war stops play,'* only to start in devastating earnest the following year in May.

Now I was grounded once again in Oxfordshire with the 'glittering prize' of Oxford ahead of me. Meanwhile I advertised to give English lessons. I had a Japanese pupil called Taki, short for Takahashi. He was very compliant and when I got a teaching job for a week, right in the Chiltern Hills, he agreed to come and stay at the pub in Peppard to get daily evening lessons. He preferred to sit on the floor and so I followed suit, to the utter amazement of the publican and his clientele, who could spy on the new teacher and the 'Jap' through the glass door to the Saloon! When we parted, he gave me a beauti-fully wrapped box of chocolates and I was crass enough to ask for my money, which was discreetly hidden inside. Forty seven years later, I was in Tokyo and found that there were masses of Takahashis in the phone book, so there was no reunion.

Chapter 9

The Dream of Oxford against the Reality of War, 1939–1942

The first two terms at Oxford passed with little or no activity on the Western Front. This was the phony war and we began to think it would last forever. During the Easter vacation I joined Yves in Paris for his seven days leave. Paris was as exciting as ever. We recaptured our student days with a visit to the Maison Franco-Britannique where Monsieur Desclos was still in charge. He was enthusing about one of his students who had risen to the rank of captain. Yves, who was still a private, waxed indignant at the fulsome praise! The war seemed irrelevant; it was almost business as usual except for some meatless days. I went home, no longer feeling so indignant about France taking the brunt of hostilities. They were ensconced on the Maginot Line feeling relatively safe.

But then came the bombshells – thousands of them – with German troops pouring through France. Refugees flooding the roads towards the south were being riddled with machine-gun bullets.

At Oxford I volunteered to take my car over to help them, but fortunately for me, poor Robin, my ancient car, did not pass muster. I must confess that I hadn't realized that the refugees were being machine-gunned; would I have volunteered then? So I threw myself into making a collection of clothes and bed linen for the destitute. But almost immediately it was all over and France was occupied. (Much later, when the war was over, I was especially moved by a film about the plight of the escaping refugees where the children who had been machine-gunned during the desperate escape from Paris were playing at burying their dolls.)

I learnt after the war that Yves had been discharged from the army straight away and had spent the war at home in Nice. This was in the so-called unoccupied Vichy zone where there was great starvation except for collaborators. By that time, over five years, I was happily married to Harry, and Yves had married an English girl so neither of us got in touch.

Marc Janin being Jewish, had joined the *Chasseurs Alpins* the moment

France was occupied to escape deportation. I learnt much later from his sister that he had suffered innumerable hardships in the high Alps and he finally returned a broken man after the war. I never saw him again. I did telephone him when I visited Paris many years later. We arranged to meet but he was in no condition to manage any relationship and he died soon afterwards. Although he escaped the death camps, he was every bit a victim. I recall him at Oxford, a brilliant pianist, full of *joie de vie* and plans for the future.

In the security of Oxford my aim was clear: to maintain the glory of France. I became the secretary of the French Club, promoting French music, French art, French theatre and especially French films, culminating in a visit of General de Gaulle at the august Sheldonian Theatre. De Gaulle was immensely tall, made even taller by his stance, bolt upright with his large nose high up in the air. In this posture he introduced himself by distributing autographed photographs of himself! We had debated who should introduce him on this memorable occasion and decided rather reluctantly on the only one of us who spoke French without a trace of accent. But he was quite a maverick and our fears were soon to be realized at his first 'tribute': *"Mon General, je ne vous aime pas."* De Gaulle's nose rose to further heights. Then came *"Je n'aime pas votre politique."* We were all on tenterhooks waiting for de Gaulle's reaction. Then, just in time, the famous words attributed to the philosopher Voltaire, rescued the essence of the *Entente Cordiale* between Britain and France. *"I disapprove of what you say, but I will defend to the death your right to say it."* We all sighed with relief. That was what we were all fighting for: Freedom.

The meeting was a great success with enthusiastic support for the Free French Cause. There was a steady flow of French students from Oxford being called up to the Free French Navy and the French Club was their focus when on leave. It was a consolation to know that there was at least some resistance from France and although co-operation between Churchill and De Gaulle was at a premium there were also French forces in North Africa.

Looking back, I feel guilty about the life we were leading at Oxford; Europe was occupied and the bombing of London had begun in real earnest. First there was the Battle of Britain which took such a toll of our young airmen who staved off the very real threat of an invasion for which we were singularly unprepared. I could never believe that this would happen to us. The personal side of the price paid was brought home to me when my friend Margaret's husband, Bill Lynes, went missing on a bombing raid over Berlin. Bill was Monty's school friend and I had introduced them. I visited Margaret and her tiny baby in the intensive care unit of the Radcliffe Hospital; she had had a miscarriage after the news of Bill's fate. The baby survived but Bill didn't.

The first realization of the horror of saturation bombing was in the autumn of 1940 when the entire centre of the city of Coventry was obliterated. The beautiful cathedral was reduced to a shell. We registered the damage even in the heavily censored newsreel but the full extent of the damage inflicted only came to me years later when I saw a film spanning that whole relentless night. By then I had suffered the unexpected shock of the V1 doodlebugs and later on, the V2 rockets. I can still remember the doodlebugs with the rasping, grating, noise they made until they were over their target. Then, as the engines cut out, there was a long silence – while we silently wished: *"go on – go away from us!"* Then came the explosion. The V2 rockets were different – suddenly there was a big explosion – the first you knew you were the target. But that was nothing like the relentless waves of thousands of bombers throughout that night in Coventry. But Oxford life went on as usual. Was this a protection or cover that inured us against our natural feelings of compassion and hardened in us our concept of the horrors of war? These realizations slowly guided me towards become a pacifist.

Later there was fierce fighting on the Eastern Front with the bitter siege of Leningrad where hundreds of thousands were starving to death. We became more and more aware of the might and determination of the Soviet Union to stand up to the German onslaught – however great the sacrifice. They were certainly bearing the brunt of this terrible war and there was a detectable feeling of relief that our forces were only deployed in North Africa and that we were not yet ready to plan the opening of the Second Front. This would have shared the burden more equally – and this is what the Soviets were urgently pressing Churchill for.

So there was a surge of interest in the Soviet Union: a glorified version to some extent, yet understandable at that moment. We realized that if Hitler had continued the invasion over the Channel, we would have been occupied – and life at Oxford and everywhere else in Britain would be as hard as in occupied France. We were lucky. Hitler decided not to invade, still hoping to make an alliance with Britain.

This view has been greatly substantiated by the release of information after fifty years about the pro-Nazi views of the Duke of Windsor, formally King Edward VIII, who abdicated from the throne to marry Wallis Simpson – *"The woman I love."* The Duke had endeared himself to the British public as the Prince of Wales, not only because of his good looks and easy manner, but he was seen as caring for the poor. I recall knowing at an early age how sympathetic he was to the plight of the Welsh miners. His philandering side and his Nazi sympathies were a dark secret known only to a chosen few of the elite.

My parents
holding Jane and
Susan, my nieces –
the twins.

It has now been revealed that he urged the government to make a pact with Hitler. He and Wallis visited Hitler in Berchtesgaden during the early part of the war. Evidence has now revealed that he was releasing valuable information to Hitler about the proposed location for the opening of the Second Front! Churchill had to release him from his liaison post in Paris to become Governor of the Bahamas – out of harm's way. This to me is a shocking example of how vital information can be kept from us, the general public.

Meanwhile, on the Home Front life went on much as usual. The bombing had more or less stopped: all German bombers were needed for the Russian Front, so there was a welcome lull. Although we had food rationing our diet was wholly adequate and in some ways, more nutritious; for example, the British loaf, which unlike the present sliced white bread, retained all its goodness. Restaurants had a limit of five shillings per meal and mostly they rallied to the occasion, although I once had a sliver of cheese that I swear I could see through! At one stage I went vegetarian and had nuts instead of meat and also nut butter. An advantage of this was that I could trade my nuts for another source of protein to provide variety; also health food stores managed to trade more unusual items which would be unrationed. Some meat and fish innovations were decidedly unpopular such as whale meat: it looked so bloody. Also the general public did not react kindly to fish with a strange name, for good reasons: they were often full of bones, although some have remained after the war as one of the cheapest choices like coley. Dried egg was a poor substitute in omelettes or scrambled, but at least it was protein. A staple meat substitute was the ubiquitous spam, which, seventy years later, is the word that denotes possible junk email, being part of the technological revolution which has beset this next century.

On the farm my brother had started bee-keeping and was allowed an extra sugar ration so I was drawn home to partake of the honey! I think he had to sell some but could consume the rest.

As students we did not feel the pinch so much, as the Colleges kept up the tradition of teas with anchovy toast and out-of-this-world cakes. There was always coffee consumed at a fashionable venue: once the Cadena, then inexplicably changing to Ellistons. What a contrast this all was to those suffering under the brutal occupation, many of them near starvation level.

Apart from study much of our time was spent listening to music on the gramophone. We always used spine or thorn needles, which we had to sharpen after every recording when Toscanini conducted; his ebullient style made him my favourite.

Our secluded life at Oxford continued. I have sweet memories of carefree punting on the Cherwell with laden picnic baskets, the peaceful deer-park at Magdalen and Christchurch Meadows, with an array of wild flowers on the site that was an inspiration for 'Alice in Wonderland.' Today, I am always aware of the suffering endured in so many other parts of the world: wars, dictatorships and starvation. I still have the belief that we shall be able to make the world a fairer place.

I had bought a warm beaver-lamb coat with my ill-gotten gains from the tourist trip to Nice (it also cost £10) so I felt all set for my new life. After an uncomfortable night spent at the home in Cowley of my mother's depressed sister Gladys, I gratefully accepted the security of Mr. Milnes' invitation to have a room at Five Mile Drive, the boundary line of North Oxford and the beginning of the countryside. Work began with considerable demands: tutorials, lectures and essays, so I spent a lot of time in the College Library realising how little I really knew of the French language and literature. We had to write one essay a week for our tutor. Women had to share their tutorial privilege with another, whereas the men had a whole hour to themselves. My first essay was a critique on the work of Rabelais, whom I was really in no position to judge. But I appreciated his outlook and still quote the famous motto inscribed on his *'Abbaye de Thélème'* – *"Fais ce que voudras"* – *"Do as thou wilt."* He had revolutionary ideas. Our studies did not include his *'Drole Stories'* that would put *'The Canterbury Tales'* to shame in their sheer sexiness.

Our tutor was Miss Hugon and she seemed never to have stirred from her easy chair. After I had read out my offering in hesitant and apologetic tones she would always say, *"Quite so, Miss Clinkard, quite so"* with the same emphasis on the ultimate syllable *'ard,'* and so I was none the wiser on her opinion of my admiration of Rabelais. Later I changed with considerable difficulty to a really dishy tutor, a Mr Hunt, who was a specialist on Balzac. We both agreed that Balzac was the greatest French novelist and had world-renown.

Another tutor was Miss Lane-Poole who looked posh and acted like her name. She took us for Latin that often stretched to the Greek myths via Virgil. I recall her sophisticated Oxford accent as she described Aeneas: *"Why couldn't he have said to Dido, darling I've simply got to go; it's a frightful nuisance but I'll be back, instead of sailing off furtively in the middle of the night without a word?"* She managed to convey modern parallels to the ancient myths.

We studied Greek mythology officially with Sir Gilbert Murray, famous for his translations of Greek drama into English. After his lectures, which went over my head to a large extent, as I was unacquainted with Sophocles and Aeschylus, he would hover amongst us benevolently asking how we enjoyed the classic Greek plays. I always feigned undue enthusiasm, although I hadn't got round to studying them. Looking back I would have been inspired by discussions on how the Greek myths were relevant to us today.

But at least he was carried away by his enthusiasm; other lecturers read out a chapter a week during the eight week terms from their own published work, usually from books conveniently composed of eight chapters. Thank goodness Greek wasn't a prerequisite, although Latin was, which caused me some distress. When I found it was a compulsory subject for Pass Mod exams in the first year, I knew I would need some tutoring to bring me up to standard – as my formidable interviewer had already expressed. I answered an advert by the Reverend Nightingale, who was righteously indignant when I asked him if he could help me with my weekly assignments. We parted company and a graduate student managed to coach me successfully through the exam.

But this was Oxford and I was thrilled to be cycling to lectures down the High Street or in St. Giles with my scanty undergraduate gown flying in the wind.

My fellow students were not my age group: they were eighteen and nineteen year-olds and I was twenty two, being as ever, a late developer. I suppose I had acquired a slight gloss of sophistication, although I really felt humble in this august institution. They had mostly come from high schools where they had studied for Higher School Certificate and then for Oxford Entrance. They had barely emerged from the schoolgirl stage and I thought them a lot of swots.

I got into quite a different set. On arrival I had contacted George who was still struggling to get a pass degree. He was under the wing of a somewhat older woman, Baptista Gilliat-Smith, daughter of a retired ambassador. Now she was really sophisticated. She sensed trouble at my reappearance and promptly invited me to a posh lunch at 'Weeks.' Waited on by the chef, we had the tenderest tournado steak I had ever tasted. I was duly impressed. She was very kind to me and said I could visit her flat any time. It was bang in the centre of Oxford in Turl Street. This was a lifeline for me as Five Mile Drive was true to its name, on the outskirts of Oxford. We even set up French tuition together which was largely patronised by students of Exeter College opposite her flat. Baptista would sit there sipping black coffee and never without a cigarette in her mouth. Later she would die of lung cancer.

I embraced the social life by joining the Labour Party. A concern for politics was beginning to stir in my mind: Leon Blum, the then Prime Minister of France, had begun to influence me with his Socialist policy, although he was being blamed by the Right for all the many problems that France was experiencing. At Oxford the first Socialist meeting I had attended was in an elegant private house with a preponderance of Indian women, resplendent in their saris. I don't think I had ever seen a sari before. But what they were saying made me most indignant: how Britain was exploiting India and how they must work to get India's freedom from the shackles of the Empire. I had always known how lucky they were to be part of our Empire on which the sun never sets! I seemed to be in a minority of one, so I kept my mouth shut and listened with growing indignation. But I wanted to soak up all that I was experiencing. Maybe today if I attended a Labour Party meeting I would still be a minority of one – with the roles reversed!

When I returned to the farm for the Christmas vacation, it was another life. I reverted to my broad Oxfordshire accent automatically or so it seemed to me. At Oxford I felt I had to cultivate the Oxford accent. I'd had enough of teasing about my 'a's' like '*baad*' at Milham Ford School, so I was halfway there. Also I had had almost a two-year gap by continually speaking French. In fact when I first returned I found that I was thinking of the French word almost subliminally and then translating it back into English. So the transition from broad Oxfordshire to a vague imitation of the posh Oxford accent was less of a jump.

The two worlds rarely overlapped, but when they did it could cause me great embarrassment. I suppose I had become a snob. Auntie Mabel and Uncle Harold drove their cart to the Oxford covered market on Wednesdays and Fridays from Toot (pronounced *Tut*) Baldon to sell their produce from their smallholding. If they spotted me they would load me with wet kisses and Uncle Harold always had a dewdrop at the end of his nose. Auntie Mabel was the robust image of Dawn French in 'Lark Rise to Candleford.' I was always careful to avoid their permanent stall when I was with one of my student friends.

There was also Sam Lewingdon, a close friend of my father, who enjoyed a shoot on our farm when he wasn't fulfilling his duties as a scout at

Christchurch. Scouts waited on their undergraduates hand and foot, even emptying their chamber pots, but Sam had his quiet dignity. He described to my father how he had spent a day repairing a clock belonging to one of his students that wouldn't work. The next morning he found it in pieces in the fireplace where his student had hurled it, presumably because of the tick. I was never sure which was his staircase when I visited Christchurch to see a friend and would have been highly embarrassed if he had served us tea. He probably would have taken it in his stride. It was a case of everyone being aware of their place in society and accepting it to a greater or lesser extent. There were also some occasions when I was invited to a student's digs and found they were the tenants of my relations, who, like so many householders, let a couple of rooms to supplement meagre salaries. My relatives were liberally spread in the city and the nearby villages and I seemed to have endless encounters with them when I was an undergraduate.

The only one of my old Elsfield playmates I ran into was Kathy (Did) Warner – the one whose friendship I had so desired when at the village school. We met outside Ellistons, the posh clothes shop where she was apprenticed in the millinery department. We had little to say to each other; the gulf was too wide to bridge. I was so glad to renew our friendship when in my eighties I got in touch with her for material for my book about growing up at Elsfield. She was a wealth of information with amusing memories of our childhood.

I have left to the end any details of my relationship with the opposite sex during my stimulating three years at Oxford. At first I was missing the companionship of Yves during much of the previous two years and my sights were already set on the possibility of his leave which would be an unexpected bonus at Easter.

After the fall of France my energies were taken up with the support for the French Club and it was only in my second year that I began to miss more regular attachments, and then for companionship rather than sexual. George was kept under close supervision by Baptista as there was more than a spark between us.

There was also Georges Desmaris, the attractive secretary of the French Club, from Mauritius. I took over his job and we spent quite a lot of time together, dining at the elite George Restaurant, coffee at Ellistons and walking in Christchurch Meadows. Then Georges was called up to join the Free French Fleet.

David Lockie was a Scottish aristocrat and I enjoyed being invited to a delicious cream tea at Magdalen College after a walk in the deer-park. He was a gifted pianist and if he became somewhat amorous I implored him to play a Brahms Rhapsody and he always succumbed. Years later I saw a fulsome account of his marriage in 'The Tatler.'

David was the only aristocrat I had any sustained relationship with. There was Michael Astor, son of the renowned Nancy Astor, the first woman M.P. from the stately home, Cliveden. I also had some acquaintance with Auberon Waugh and felt quite indignant when he said glibly, *"You really must come to breakfast some time,"* an invitation I knew he had no intention of honouring. In both cases the idea of the different plane of the 'gentry' had been imbued in my psyche, ever since my village childhood with John Buchan as our Lord of the Manor at Elsfield.

By 1941 call-up papers came thick and fast and I found myself forging a more permanent relationship with Tony Sutton. He was younger than me and would be called up in 1942, the year when I would take my degree. He was at Exeter College, sited opposite Baptista's flat in Turl Street, and we had met there for Italian lessons with the versatile Baptista.

This friendship gradually took on that sense of security I always cared for, especially in my third year when there was so much work to be done. We shared a great taste for the arts and for languages and our favourite treat was to take the train to London, enjoy a continental restaurant meal at Pruniers in Soho and then go on to the opera at Covent Garden. By 1941 London was swinging: the bombing had more or less stopped. It was a life of contrasts with endless essays on the one hand and on the other, enjoyment of the creative world of art and music, always with a partner to share the social life.

I kept in close contact with my parents and my brother Monty. Joy, his wife, was now living with them and had by now produced the twins, Jane and Susan. I still had 'Robin,' my diminutive Singer car and could make frequent visits to the family farm, 'Marylands' in Chislehampton. There, I would fall into the Oxfordshire brogue talking with my father while my mother cooked in the country tradition – which remained my favourite kind of food.

I invited her to tea in Tony's rooms and when she finally settled down comfortably in a capacious leather armchair she beamed at Tony and said confidingly *"Our Mil 'ud get anywhere!"* The turn of speech went down in our history. This forecast was fulfilled in her eyes when she and my father sat in the auspicious Sheldonian Theatre to see me, cap and gowned, taking my degree. So my two lives were joined – a brief link between farm and university.

My finals were rapidly approaching and I took a few days out at the farm to prepare myself. Then I did a very silly thing. The twins were having their vaccination against smallpox and, as mine had not taken when I was a baby, I was offered a shot. Disaster! I woke up on the first day of the exams with a thigh as big as a full-size leg of mutton and a temperature of 104 degrees! The authorities were less than sympathetic. I must attend otherwise my degree would be null and void. There was no such thing as aegrotat. My family came to the rescue. Father jumped in the car, drove me to Oxford wrapped in a blanket and deposited me at the Taylorian Institute where the exams were held. Luckily it was near the parks, where he watched the cricket until he called for me and took me back to the farm. And so it continued for the whole of the ten days. My father had come once more to the rescue, just as he had when I was a child, on his white horse, when I couldn't get down from the oak tree.

As ever I went back to the farm for the vacation where time seemed to have stayed still. It was always a retreat into another life that I assumed spontaneously – before the reality of my call-up closed in.

Chapter 10

Called Up to Teach, 1942–1944

After three exhilarating years at Oxford, the dream world was over and real life had to be faced. It was made abundantly clear to me that my compulsory war work was to be a teacher. This was far removed from my romantic visions of being a spy that had been part of my passion to do something for conquered France. A routine interview for Chatham House, the political think tank, had put paid to that ambivalent aspiration. One of my co-students in Paris might have been part of the liaison with the resistance. I had travelled with him on my journey to Berlin. Many years later I heard his name, Kenneth MacKenzie, mentioned in a television programme on the brave volunteers of the SOE (Special Operations Executive) secretly parachuted into occupied France.

So my life was transformed from the dizzy days of Oxford to the reality of getting a teaching post. Before Tony's call-up, we spent a blissful fortnight together in Torquay, where tourists still had access to the sea, unlike the resorts on the Channel coastline. There was a notice in the local paper advertising for a teacher of French, English and Latin at the Torquay Boys' Grammar School. I thought it would be pleasant to live at the seaside and applied for the job. I was successful – which was hardly surprising as this was summer 1942 and most of the male teachers had been called up. I was then marooned in a basement bed-sit (or rather sofa-bed) a mile from the school. Accommodation was hard to find. At least Torquay was a haven from bombing raids. Then began another period of loneliness – just like the training college days; what a contrast from Paris, Nice and Oxford. I had never been used to catering for myself and was grateful for a plateful of roast dinner handed down by the sister of the landlord. This 'manna' from upstairs was summarily put to a stop by the landlord's wife. She obviously wondered where would it end? It did – all too soon from my point of view. I hadn't realized how wet Devon was, in particular, Torquay. This was brought home to me during the first day at the school: a huge puddle covered the whole of the entrance to the hut in the playground, my allotted classroom for twelve year-olds. The only way I could enter the class was to take a flying leap over the

Wartime marriage with my wartime hairstyle.

puddle area, with my new BA gown floating out behind me – rather like Superman, much to the amusement of my new pupils. We established a good relationship. They were all successful recipients of the eleven-plus exam and therefore a privileged selection of 18% of the total school population. They were prepared to give this new school a go and so they were quite a pleasure to teach and I began to enjoy it.

Tony and I thought that it would be a guarantee of our relationship if we married before he was sent overseas. We felt that leave on compassionate grounds might then be easier. His parents, owners of Suttons Jewellery business, thought I was 'jewellery-digging' and they opposed the marriage and took us to court – as Tony was just under twenty one. This made us all the more determined. We won and the Torquay local paper had the headlines, '*Wins right to marry teacher!*' Strangely enough my in-class discipline didn't suffer. There was a 'do as you like' atmosphere in the air caused, I am sure, by the war. It reminded me again of Rabelais's adage, '*Fais ce que voudras:*' that was spreading as the war progressed. We were supported by a lawyer who was a Methodist and he organized our simple wedding. The preacher was called Victor Tudor, and when he escorted me home after the services leading up to the wedding it always ended in a not altogether chaste kiss, with a warning not to mention it to the lawyer – *"He wouldn't understand."*

Soon after we were married, Tony was drafted overseas to Italy and I settled down to enjoy teaching. The staff all welcomed me in their distinctive ways and several of them invited me to join them. The most disastrous was for tea with the devout headmaster's wife – they were both equally devout. After homemade cake she got down to business and I found myself on my knees imbibing her prayers. I seem to recall that I sent a note of thanks but

On holiday on Newquay beach.

recanting any apparent conversion. Her husband made excuses to me: it was all very embarrassing. The Science teacher had a more mystic approach: he was a spiritualist and I feared being roped in to a table-tapping session as I drank my glass of cold water. Luckily he contented himself by giving graphic descriptions of the haunting presence of bodies from the other world.

Other overtures were straightforward: the Spanish teacher had no difficulty in corralling me into his classes. Mrs Humphrey was the English teacher; I enjoyed her homemade cakes with no strings attached and listened to Brahms's Fourth Symphony. I am listening to it now as I write and I recollect how lonely I was, saying to myself, *"It won't always be like this"* in the third triumphal movement – and it wasn't.

But I did find the grammar school curriculum restrictive in keeping each subject in its particular little box, whereas my ideas inclined towards a more holistic approach. I was greatly influenced by the writings of John Dewey, an American educationist who favoured an approach of "learning by doing." This was unknown to the conventional version of following slavishly the sequence of lessons whether English, Latin or French. When the headmaster told me he was going to sit in on my Latin lesson, in panic I chose to go over the one I had taught the day before. Nobody noticed!

I soon had a good friend on the staff, Molly. Her mother however, summed me up – I could tell. She indicated that 'her Molly' should not be influenced by such a creature. I began to realize that this part of the world was often under the influence of many sects including strict Baptists. Theirs was a stricter code of morals than I had been used to. For example when we tried to organize an 'American Supper Party' at the school for young teachers it was forbidden! Probably the word 'American' aroused deep fears; also the publicity was on bright green paper!

Life ticked on apace with a holiday at Easter in Newquay with Molly, whose mother had grudgingly allowed her to associate with the likes of me. I loved walking along the long sandy seaside where tidal waves came crashing on to the beach. We shared a table with a newly-married couple on leave. It

Me and my Mother on her visit to Torquay.

was as though the war had been put on hold. We even had a fried egg and a rasher of bacon each and the new husband waxed eloquently about his wife's cooking, starting every sentence with, *"My wife."* Maybe he was one of the men who finally invaded France on D-Day.

Back in Torquay there was little reminder of the war other than the rations. It was a haven from bombing raids. Very occasionally we had experi-enced a 'tip and run raid,' when the boys were ordered to duck under the doubtful protection of their desks. As they all had full inkwells it seemed an appropriate moment to spill these in the confusion of the emergency. For the boys this was a welcome incident to interrupt the tedium of the lessons.

One positive feature of my first job was the incredible beauty of the coun-tryside: the red rocks and cliffs with undulating paths overlooking the sea at Babbacombe, the estuary at Dartmouth, and the picturesque fairytale villages hidden between minor roads and high hedges. But a holiday atmosphere was not for me and I longed to enjoy the glamour of London. The Blitz had finally ended and the threats of the V1's and V2's were yet to be envisaged. There was a tendency to forget the war when it wasn't taking its toll directly. Then a new relationship came into my life (after a year)!

The Yanks came to Devon: they were 'overpaid, oversexed and over here.' Al Warren was a committed communist and he revived my interest that had been kindled at Oxford. We met frequently at John Burns, the History teacher's house, and I found the discussions stimulating, especially the topic of the struggle that was being waged on the Russian Front. This was well before the long-awaited D-Day. There was a growing conviction that the Western powers were only too glad to let the Nazis and the Soviets destroy each other while confining themselves to the North African campaign. Later in early 1944 in London, I would be joining the protesters with the chant, *"Open the Second Front now!"* There was a tendency to forget the bloody success of El Alamein in North Africa and the heroic campaign of the navy in the Atlantic in comparison with the Eastern Front.

Once more I had a boyfriend and the loneliness vanished. I seemed to be able to sustain a year's separation from the love of my life and then some change took place leading to a new relationship. Was it the effect of the war? There was certainly a departure from the more rigid standards before the war when much that was going on had to be hidden in the back row of the cinema or in the confines of the back of a small car. I feel that I can't blame the war for my inability to remain steadfast after twelve months of faithfulness. The rigidly compulsory nature of my workload shrouded by the dismal effect of the blackout, were definitely contributory factors. Just as I finally forgot Yves stuck in occupied France without any means of communication, so now I found that Al was replacing Tony who was in Tobruk on the North African campaign.

I knew that I wasn't the only one who had fallen for a Yank who would bring romance, nylons and ice cream into our drab wartime lives. But I didn't realize that twice as many illegitimate babies were born during the war years; presumably the increase could be partly due to the American contribution.

Life became fascinating with dancing at the Imperial Hotel and exploration of the Devon countryside, with new ideas to be discussed in the welcome atmosphere of John Burns' hospitable home where Communism was the order of the day. Al and I finally celebrated Christmas at the Cornish seaside village of Mousehole, pronounced *'Muzzle.'*

I decided to move to London. Al was likely to be posted anywhere in Britain and no train journey was too long to join him at the weekend. The desolate dark journeys in the blackout were a small price to pay for the love and companionship that followed. It was easy to get a job and I went for two interviews: one at Hampton and the other, the City of London School for Girls. As the suburban train bore me further and further away from the centre of London, I decided that Hampton was not for me and made my lame excuses on the station platform – much to the dismay of the disappointed master of the Boys Grammar School who had come to collect me. I took the next train back to the city with enthusiasm – back to the throbbing heart of London. Considering that I was due to teach elementary German at Hampton, when I had planned to be one chapter ahead of every lesson, they were fortunate not to have employed me.

I was quite confident about getting the post of French teacher at the august City of London School for Girls. This is where I wanted to be: at the centre of things. It was January 1944 and the Blitz had died down – apart from the V-1 and V-2 bombs that summer. The school was then in Carmelite Street, off

Teaching in the City of London during the V bomb attacks.

Fleet Street; on one side of the road was the endless throb of the printing press of the Evening Standard, and on the opposite side were the powerful voices of the Guildhall School of Music. Both seemed to converge on my classroom creating a cacophony of noise. Straining my voice, I tried to keep to my policy of teaching only in French.

It was surprisingly difficult to find accommodation in London as all the evacuees had returned. The fighting had become even more fierce on the Eastern Front and in bitter cold, Leningrad was still holding out under the most stringent conditions of starvation. I finally found a room with Queenie, a Communist Party member, in the then slums of North Kensington. So once again, I seemed to be leading a triple life: working in the very establishment-setting of the City of London School, and as Communist activist after school, and weekend romance with an American soldier. There was always the pressure, mixed with inspiration, to be politically active in the Communist Party: in our respective unions; on marches relevant to our aims and general support for our local community. We also supported the Labour Party, but were always convinced that sooner or later Social democrats would relinquish their vision of Socialism – which they did years later with New Labour.

My work changed when they asked me to be in charge of the second form: eight to eleven year-olds. I was then able to try out my new ideas of an integrated education. But I had more enthusiasm than experience. To complete the large model house we were building in the basement, I had to bring in a carpenter friend to put things right after school – under cover of the blackout. As a local project we explored London: the colourful markets: one especially stands out: Smithfield meat market where we had to wear overcoats and keep at a brisk pace, as it was below freezing. We visited the House of Commons and met the local MP, a true blue of the City of London, so my politics had to be kept secret. We also adopted a naval ship and entertained the Captain who was delighted to meet the children who had followed the ship's progress and written letters to the crew.

The highlight of these expeditions was on a foggy afternoon – and there were continual thick pea soup fogs in those days, described so vividly in Dickens' 'Great Expectations.' We were walking along the Embankment on our way back to school when we were overtaken by the lamplighter. He had a long pole with a blazing light on the end and went at lightening speed. My crocodile quickened its pace to match – rather like a horse when being over-taken by another. So there we were, trotting at full speed, only pausing for a brief moment while each lamp post became bathed in a misty glow. These were the wartime days of the blackout, so anything brighter would not be allowed. Was it gaslight? It certainly responded to a mere touch of the lighted pole. It was right at the end of an era of gas-lighting and my pupils were thrilled to participate. At least I was practicing my ideas of enlightened educa-tion: in a nutshell it was a creative approach to the enjoyment of learning, free from innumerable examinations and league tables. It was much more exper-imental than teaching French, although I did apply the direct conversational method and this was the language I loved.

There was one bonus in teaching in the City of London School during the war; that was to be honoured with the status of being a Free Woman of the City of London. I gathered this gave me the right to drive a flock of sheep over Westminster Bridge and to live in one of the City's alms houses in my old age! I have not taken advantage of either of these benefits yet.

Then finally the day that we had been waiting for so eagerly: the Second Front in June 1944 and Al was one of the first to land on the Normandy beaches. I was once more alone. The blackout seemed darker than ever, the little bed-sit provided no solace and I lost some of my enthusiasm for the Communist Party activities. I needed a partner. Even when the war in Europe was brought to an end on VE day, 8th May 1945, it didn't fulfill the delirious ecstasy that I had expected. Nevertheless the immense burden of war was released from my shoulders. I went on my own that day to an open-air Communist Party celebration to listen to a speech by our local party secretary: an inappropriate diatribe against Capitalism as opposed to Communism, when it was the moment to celebrate the victory. But apparently someone in our small crowd had spotted me. It was Harry.

Chapter 11

Harry and the Communist Party, 1945 and beyond...

After the dark times of loneliness: blackout and bombs and war, teaching by day and political work at weekends, there suddenly appeared a shaft of light at the end of the tunnel. The first glimpse of Harry was of a handsome young man as he came into a Communist Party Social, carrying a young toddler horizontally on his hip. I was fascinated enough to find out to know that it wasn't his offspring, but belonged to a Norwegian comrade.

So Harry and I were destined to meet. He had spotted me at the VE celebrations. I too had mentally earmarked him, then circumstances beyond our control arranged for us to meet each other. Harry had come from the North of England and was now a member of the Notting Hill Group that met with us slum dwellers of Ladbroke Grove. Our groups were often called cells, which to me had a distasteful connotation of conspiracy. Soon I eagerly anticipated the branch meetings that were held regularly on Friday nights. I had promptly joined the North Kensington Group of the Communist Party as soon as I moved to London. It was a run-down area, ready for support – if not conversion. The latter was wishful thinking, as the great British public, primed with capitalist conviction, was justifiably cautious. I myself felt that if I sold them pamphlets, it might give them space for thought. I recall selling 'A History of the Chinese Student Movement' to some bewildered occupant of Peabody Buildings and I didn't realise they were simply paying me to play in the next street!

No, I didn't enjoy the Sunday morning canvassing. There was certainly a lot of pressure to canvas from the hierarchy in our little group. These were the devotees: proletarians whose lives were dedicated to 'The Cause.' This pressure was contributory in leading us belatedly to question the whole ethos of the Communist Party of Great Britain. We left it in 1956 after the Soviet invasion of Hungary when we were finally convinced of the evil policies of the Soviet Union. I must add that it didn't lessen our ideals of justice and a more equal society. With the gap between rich and poor ever-widening not only in Britain but all over the world, my feelings remain as strongly as ever, but the

Harry Masheder.

path to achieve a fairer society seems more desirable but more complex than ever; with conflict resolution rather than revolution, which we never supported.

The feeling of belonging was the great attraction to someone like me living in a tiny bed-sit in blackout London. I was always there on Friday night and that provided me with a chance for my romance with Harry to develop. There were marches when we would all congregate in Trafalgar Square and experience that deep feeling of comradeship that is so nourishing to the human soul.

I did however reluctantly sell the Daily Worker on the same spot each week and gave a horrified denial when one of my pupils asked if she'd seen me there!

When I moved to Hampstead, the party cell was more of an intellectual kind and almost all of them were Jewish people from the East End and refugees from Hitler's Germany in the thirties. They formed the greater number of my close friends for the rest of our lives. Some had fought in the Spanish war against Franco's fascism. We all maintained our strong sense of justice, but we all left the Party over the years that followed.

When it was decided that I should take over Harry's job as 'Lit Sec' and he would assume the reigns of 'Soc Soc,' which had been my role in organising social events, he proposed that we should discuss this transfer over dinner at a Swiss restaurant in Soho.

I arrived dolled up to the nines with an anticipatory smile, which gradually faded during the course of a whole hour's wait. I was finally giving way to despair, when Harry rushed in with the same sort of excuse that I was destined to receive during our fifty years together. Our relationship soon began to be extended beyond our mutual political activities, and Harry invited me to spend the weekend with friends of his in the Midlands' countryside. They were Tony and Wilf Stevenson. Tony was a paraplegic who had made a lot of money on a liquid fertilizer based on seaweed. Years later, he apparently fell accidentally to his death from an overhanging branch into the swift stream below. Fortunately he was well-insured so his widow was well provided for.

The weekend spent with the Stevensons was charged with high emotion between the two of us but it finally consolidated our relationship. Somehow I had omitted to tell Harry that I was still married to Tony Sutton and that he had been in the African Campaign for almost three years and that I was still married. Harry was devastated to hear that I was already married especially as he was in a reserved occupation designing fighter aircraft for immediate production and therefore not in active service. He felt that he could not intervene in a serviceman's marriage, although I reassured him that my marriage had ended over two years ago. But when he heard that Al had superseded Tony after a year's separation, Harry realized it was a free for all – and could take his chances! Soon a letter had to be written to Al who had been on the Western Front for the past year. Again I had held out for a whole twelve dreary months! I felt badly about it but I said to myself that I never cheated on any of them – until after a year's fidelity I had to write to them to say there was someone else. I hadn't been able to let Yves know as there was no communication with the occupied countries until the end of the war. I learnt after the war from Charles and Pierette that Yves had married an English girl and later became fat, probably owing to food deprivation during the war. I saw Charles and Pierette many years later; their joyful youth had been crushed by the hardships of the occupation. They told me then that Yves had died. Pierette was very ill with cancer and Charles from heart trouble and after our one meeting in Cannes there was no response to my letters.

As for Al, he was philosophical; we both knew that because of our communist politics, we would not be able to live together in the States. During the war in 1944 I had naively applied for a post war visa and had been cursorily rejected by the American Consulate. I even tried to convert them to socialism! The persecution of anyone who might have had communist or socialist sympathies was already in hand in the States and came to full fruition during the pernicious McCarthy Trials in the early fifties, when many of the Left were imprisoned or were blacklisted and so deprived of their livelihood, especially those in the film industry. There was a certain irony that our divorce finally came through naming Al as the co-respondent, although he couldn't be traced to pay for it. He wrote afterwards from California saying he was happily married and was the father of twins, which he thought was a great joke!

From then on London life with Harry was blissful: I had the companionship I always craved for. We were full of the delights of peace on VJ day on 15th August 1945. We celebrated not by joining the crowds outside Buckingham Palace but by going to the countryside in Kent. I recall singing together seated on the grassy slopes, strangely enough, without any self-consciousness; the song was full of joy: *"The Apple Tree!"* We then found a delightful bed and breakfast in an idyllic village called Eynesford. Harry actually wrote a poem about it and I caught this glimpse of it over his bashful shoulder; it was in a sort of mediaeval English featuring '*Eynesforde.*' We started to make plans to live there, but the prospect of commuting daily to the City of London School and Napiers, where Harry designed aircraft, respectively brought us back to reality. But London, explored anew in our euphoria, was still our first love. And we experienced it to the full: theatres, special cinemas, like The Academy and Studio One showed French films; days out in the country, walks in the parks, rallies in Trafalgar Square; even the Opera, which left Harry utterly bemused after tasting '*Il Trovatore!*'

The latter was an attraction I organised for the 'Young Teachers Association' – '*London by Night.*' I was an enthusiastic member of the National Union of Teachers and the London branch was a bit more progressive than Devon, which had been such a backwater. There was always however a hard core of older teachers that regarded young teachers with suspicion. I argued hard for the abolition of the eleven-plus in the 1944 Education Act. This was successful, but our proposal to limit the size of the new comprehensive schools to five hundred pupils rather than over two thousand did not get ratified. Years later I became a founder member of Human Scale Education, an inspiration from '*Small is Beautiful,*' and at last, smaller units in the large comprehensives are being introduced. It is difficult for young pupils of twelve years-old not to feel alienated amongst two thousand others and this limited reform is still in its infancy.

More than these day-to-day activities, I recall the holidays Harry and I had together. One was to the Isle of Arran, off the Scottish coast near Glasgow. It seemed like another country with its hedges of bright red fuschias, but it still had the tell-tale drizzle of the West Coast. We set up our little tent in the meadows adjoining White Water Glen, which sparkled with white spray as it dashed around the boulders of the mountain, entitled ominously Goat Fell. Our most vivid memory is centred round this luscious landscape. We soon made plans to climb to the top of Goat Fell, but our timing was way out and it wasn't until we had finished our 'white' steak lunch that we set off. In an effort to keep the meat cool, Harry had secured the steak in the fast flowing stream and was astonished to discover that it had assumed the pristine white of the spray so we thought we had better eat it! It was tasteless.

We reached the summit to see a radiant sunset and then with tropical speed, darkness fell. I think the sound of White Water Glen must have guided our faltering footsteps on the way down as we finally arrived on the side of the stream opposite to our tent. How to cross? We had surprisingly, a box of matches and Harry decided we should venture on to the rocks lit by striking them as he guided me across. Unfortunately the first match stuck to his finger and with a cry he overbalanced into the icy-cold, mountain water! Memory then draws a veil. We must have waded across, feeling our way through the rocks and somehow dried ourselves in the warmth of the tent.

We had no ill effects and the holiday was a great success. Unfortunately our overloaded rucksack was rifled in the luggage van on the way home and Uncle Jim's silver flask was taken. This led to family repercussions. Mother rightly blamed me; it made Auntie Gladys' depression worse and Uncle Jim was justifiably angry. Never borrow from relations.

The years after the war were a desperately hard time for my parents: they had had to quit their farm and sell up everything: livestock and machinery. Sir Charles Peers, Lord of the Manor of Chislehampton, had given the whole village a year's notice. My parents were now living in an abandoned farmhouse at Sescot near the river Cherwell, half a mile down from the hill at Elsfield. While they were there, Auntie Gladys, mother's favourite sister, committed suicide after years of depression. I could not help feeling pangs of guilt at not being able to comfort my mother. Her continual depression had always weighed heavily on me and although I always tried to invite her to stay and share a portion of my life, it was more from a sense of duty and pity rather than devoted filial love. So I felt I had to escape into my own world.

Escape! That is what Harry and I both wanted; Harry from his possessive, neurotic father and me from my mother. Also Harry's complete estrangement from his mother, who blamed him unjustly for the break up of her marriage, was a source of great distress for him. For me, I always had the enduring support of my father's love and mine for him. But it took the best part of my life to realize that escape is not the answer to our problems: they have to be faced.

Meanwhile escape was grasped with open arms by both of us: with peace there was escape from the sorrows of war; the bombing and the blackout and the grief of occupied Europe. At last we could visit my beloved France, but I'm afraid, not to my erstwhile beloved fiancé. We chose to go to the Isle du Levant, off Toulon in the South of France. Before we went Harry was busy making a pair of sandals for me in bright red and green suede. Unfortunately in our scatty way we left them behind and phoned to ask a friend to forward the parcel to France. Of course they never arrived and I'm sure some survivor of the occupation enjoyed them. The fact that postal services would still be in disarray immediately after the war hadn't dawned on us which showed our ignorance of the complete disruption in occupied countries.

Anyhow we finally arrived at Toulon and caught the boat to the Isle du Levant. I had always thought of the Mediterranean as a duck pond, but this crossing revealed a capacity to heave and swell equal to any storm in the Atlantic. We rose and dipped to such depths that at any moment I thought we would be overcome by the height of the waves. Dry land was salvation!

After filling our emptied stomachs with pasta, we made our way to the sweltering beach below. It was a steep descent and half way down I said to Harry *"It's funny the tricks played by the hot sun. I could have sworn that all those people sun-bathing were completely naked."* They were! We hadn't realized that the Isle du Levant was a notorious nudist colony. All eyes were upon us as we furtively made our way to some space between the bronzed bodies. I was wearing last year's tennis frock and ancient sandals and Harry was in trousers and heavy shoes and socks. We looked at each other and automatically began to undress. It wouldn't have been so bad if my tennis frock hadn't stuck half way through, showing a wriggly white bottom as I strived to get free!

At last there we were, in my beloved France under the Midi sun. Aye, there's the rub: within ten minutes we were lobster red and had ignominiously to seek the little shelter that was available from the rocks. Some of the god-like figures, apparently immune from the sun's rays, came over to engage us in conversation: *"What did you feel?"* as it was obvious that the nudity had been a great surprise. We soon became used to the nude bodies even if our burning skin had to take shelter for the whole holiday. The only image I found some-what distasteful was of a rather plump young man who seemed to take pleasure in our discomfort. He wore a paisley kerchief round his neck and brandished an aggressive pipe. One of our acquaintances was a military man who always sat bolt upright, cross-legged with his testicles popping out from time to time. A lasting friend was Solange. She had just discovered her husband making love to another woman after she had taken their three year-

Harry and myself in the High Tatras, Slovakia, 1947.

old for a swim. They beat a hasty retreat, so she left her daughter asleep in their tent and joined us in our hotel. At the end of the week we accompanied Solange to stay at her flat in Paris and there was Jacques looking very sheepish with their daughter, Mireille! I believe he never did that again. Some years later we stayed with them in Nantes and they had five thriving children, so he had sublimated his desires! Many years later I revisited Paris and found that she had died.

Our next venture was in 1947 when we went to the World Youth Festival in Prague, in what was then Czechoslovakia. The whole festival was Soviet-influenced, but I do not recall any direct indoctrination. Of course the programme contained cultural events as promoted by the Soviet Union such as the ballet from the world renowned Mariinsky Theatre of Leningrad. However what we did sense was a feeling of unease and foreboding amongst the Czechoslovak people. This was before the February coup in 1948. We set off from Victoria Station; the machinations of world politics were far from our minds. We were more concerned about my fellow teachers, Eric and Neville Bray whose rucksack had been stolen when they left it to go to the toilet. We wouldn't be so trusting today, nor would it have been allowed for fear of bombs. They were our friends and during the holiday we shared as much as we could with them.

Fortunately we were not fully aware that the journey was likely to take four days and nights. It did. Once we had left the familiar territory of France the train kept stopping, sometimes for half an hour, sometimes for hours on end. The countryside was forested and we gradually ventured out of the train and into the woods. Eventually the inevitable happened: two of our party were left behind wearing only shorts and sandals. I was duly concerned as their visas were incorporated in my passport. I needn't have worried: they had had a marvelous time, having amazingly found their way to the British Embassy in Prague, which lent them money, clothes, passes and everything else they needed to proceed to the Festival.

The four days finally passed and I recall savoring what I felt was the best meal of my life: scallop of veal, fresh vegetables and out-of-this-world desert, all washed down with the ice cold Pilsner lager in a shady garden setting. We were with our cherished friends, Ric and Peggy, who were destined later to have a tumultuous marriage.

The six of us had planned to visit the High Tatra Mountains in Slovakia before the festival began and we camped in the luscious lowlands with a challenging mountain above us. We had never seen so many raspberry bushes laden with red and yellow ripe fruit. We had fun in making a raspberry 'compote' which consisted of alternate pounding to reduce the fruit to a jelly to the rhythmic chants of a tom-tom.

We might have thought that we were in a primitive society but in fact there was a funicular to the top of the mountain for tourists. We seemed to hunt in pairs and when the other couples had left to toil to the summit, Harry and I soared up in the powerful lift. It was worth the sacrifice of our need for exercise for, as we ascended, a golden eagle with the sun reflecting light from its radiant feathers flew hovering above us. I'm afraid we rather boasted unduly about this unique image to cover up our guilt. The next day we did attempt the climb but we chose to take a short cut up the springy grassy slopes with the odd tree for shade. Gradually the lone trees turned into a thorny thicket on all sides. We were reduced to scrambling on to the brambly tops that extended as far as the eye could see. Just as we were deciding to make a hasty descent down the mountain, a black cloud descended upon us. We had disturbed a tranquil nest of hornets who protested violently against our unexpected intrusion. Torn and stung we reached safety by scaling the flat, prickly tops of the brambles. Harry and I were both rebels and this incident of defying the established way of doing things often led us into incidents such as this!

So we were ready to savour the festival. The highlight was certainly the Leningrad ballet company: a tribute to the cultural life of the Soviet Union. The performers had the custom of applauding themselves at the end, which was well-deserved. There was also Russian folk dance with Cossacks kicking in high boots and women in long skirts who seemed to be gliding round in circles.

We were invited to meet a Czech family and they confirmed our first impression of an atmosphere of pending unease. They told us of their strong sense of foreboding. Their fears turned out to be well founded. Not long afterwards, in spring 1948, the Foreign Minister, Jan Masaryk, fell to his death from the bathroom of his fourth floor apartment at the Ministry and the word went round that it was suicide, obviously circulated by collaborationists in the Soviet coup. We were not aware of the Cold War and the totalitarian nature of Stalin's regime. It was to be some years before we were completely disillusioned and left the Communist Party.

Before we went I was determined to have a swim in the Vltava. It was very hot and quite crowded on the 'beach' our side of the river. I, of course, had to distinguish myself by swimming right over to the other bank. People were waving as I looked back and I felt rather proud of myself: it was a wide river. When I finally swam back I was told that they were waving to warn me I was swimming into the sewage area! .

Leaving our new Czech friends to what was to be their fate, we boarded the train for the long trek back. Things had improved so there were no unscheduled flights into the woods. We had all bought cheap thermos flasks to store hot drinks and very soon there were sounds of the smashing of glass coming from all the compartments. The glistening silver of the thermoses had not sustained the least touch as they had no protective cover! We were thankful to get back home.

The ecstasy of peace had not worn off when the prospect of another separation found us. We were enjoying a French film at the Academy Cinema when Harry inexplicably passed me a note. I waited until the lights went up to read it and to my despair it was Harry's call-up paper. But the war was over! There had to be occupation forces in Germany and it transpired that his stint would last for three years. Of course it was only fair to share the burden and Harry being engaged in fighter aircraft design had not been exposed to any

Opposite: Harry and myself on our wedding day.

Wedding Day: Me, Harry, our parents and my brother, Monty, and my sister-in-law Joy and the twins, Susan and Jane.

fighting, only the bombing. Could I survive three years in Germany or alternatively endure separation? Unfortunately I sensed the answer to be no to the latter question, much as I loved him. We decided to get married as soon as my decree nisi came through.

The ceremony was at Hampstead Town Hall just attended by my parents and brother Monty, his wife Joy, Harry's father, Bill and his new wife, Kathleen. As shown in the wedding photograph, I was decked out in the latest fashion: a rust-brown militaristic costume, an upturned halo hat and a lacy turquoise blouse.

We borrowed a friend's flat for the reception and I found myself shopping for salad before the ceremony and I recall thinking as I queued up how strange it was that I was going to be married in an hour. Somehow it all came together in spite of five extra comrades who accepted the invitation at the last minute. There we were – our families and friends partaking of father's home-cured ham and fraternizing happily in spite of our widely different ideologies. On the basis of our philosophy of equality of the sexes, the comrades clamoured for a speech from me, just when I was finally relaxing over the potent sherry trifle!

It was a reluctant, nondescript speech that makes me blush to recall. However the guests' interest was soon diverted by Bill's experimental efforts to boil potatoes in a brand new pressure cooker which was our wedding present.

Weekend in Paris (with Harry taking the photo): ready to become a parent.

After it had emitted several explosions he turned it off, to reveal rather soft potatoes pierced with metal spikes, presumably from the lead lining of the utensil. There were understandably no takers. In any case, we were all replete.

Somehow we cleaned up and managed to catch the fast train to Dorset arriving at eleven thirty in the evening! As it was far too late to reach our booked cottage retreat, we prevailed upon Eric and Nev's parents in Sidmouth. Perhaps it was a reward from sharing everything with them when their rucksack was stolen: the parents certainly came up trumps. We were ravenous and did full justice to a fish pie and a long sleep in. And we were married at last!

It was time for a change: Harry had finally been released from his call-up, having obtained a reserved job in 'International Combustion,' a title which would surely be suspected of nurturing terrorists nowadays! I was beginning to feel 'broody'; I had spent six years teaching at the City of London School and I had begun to have this strong desire to have a child.

I gave in my notice and we went on a camping holiday to Italy and there I decided I would conceive. I was certain that my body would respond to nights on the sandy beach, the full moon and the gentle lapping of the waves of the Mediterranean. Meanwhile being lulled into a sense of security about the new life that we were sure lay ahead of us, we proceeded to savour the daytime delights of the resort of Levanto on the Italian Riviera which was recovering from the devastation of the Second World War. The local Italian comrades were thrilled to meet us and to exchange experiences. They were at last liberated from Mussolini's fascist regime and had suffered during the war that had been waged by Italians and Germans throughout the length of Italy. We profited from their excessive hospitality, as the offered beds were far more comfortable than the sand. Perhaps we compensated by giving them an outlook on the world perspective including of course, recognition of our debt to the USSR. It was to be a long time before we had the full realization of the depths of what was an evil dictatorship, far removed from our ideals of greater equality and justice.

Back in London another reality dawned. To my astonishment I was not pregnant and dramatically deplored the fact that I would be childless! But that was not before Harry had been to the sterility clinic. He would recount how he was greeted with the curt order, *"Trousers down!"* He was cleared. Then my GP suggested a weekend at a pleasant hotel and we chose the Old Brompton Grange on the road from Oxford to London. For us it was palatial. I just recall the delight of having breakfast with cornflakes. I was quite used to cornflakes for breakfast but this seemed special. Indeed it was! I was going to have Manon in nine month's time and then Suzanna arrived a couple of years later. These two events have been the best that have ever happened to me and I am everlastingly grateful to be blessed to have reached ninety four and hope to give them my love in more years to come.

POSTSCRIPT

Moving Towards Pacifism

Looking back at these memories I am struck by the insidious effect that the imminence of war had on me: the growing threat during my teenage years and then the harsh reality when I was in my early twenties.

Born during the last years of the First World War, I grew up being unaware of the intense desolation it caused. In both wars my father and brother had been, as farmers, in a reserved occupation so there was no direct experience of the appalling horrors that wars can cause. Only my Uncles were affected: Uncle Jack, who was always chesty after a gas attack behind the lines, and Uncle Tubb who remained stone-deaf. (Uncle Arthur was called Uncle 'Tubb' after he had teased my father with the nickname, 'Barrel.' My father's retaliation stuck!)

So although my family shared the nation's mistrust of Germans, it was not extended to individuals. Mr Gatz from Beckley and the one possessor of a car for hire was highly regarded and trusted by my parents to take us to our grand-parents every Christmas Day.

It wasn't until my late teenage years that I felt the heavy threat of war hanging over me, like a black thunder cloud. At first we could treat it roman-tically with myths about the First World War: volunteering to go out to nurse our wounded boyfriends!

But the reality of Hitler's Germany was dawning upon us and we were finally faced with the choice of keeping our pledge to Czechoslovakia, which Germany was about to invade. The Prime Minister Neville Chamberlain then intervened with a treaty with Hitler proclaiming *'Peace in our time'* brandishing what turned out to be, a worthless piece of paper, betraying our integrity. There was a palpable feeling of relief – the nation had been saved! I could go back to France where I was convinced my heart was captured. It was a dangerous postponement for a year when Poland, our next ally, was sched-uled for attack and we then declared war on September 3rd, 1939.

This is not the place to explore the factors that led to the Second World War but I am now convinced that many of them, not least the crippling Treaty of Versailles, could have been prevented. But long before this realization, I had to live through five years of war.

I only experienced the bombing of the V1's and V2's, which was more than enough for me. I swear I could hear my knees knocking against each other before I got to the shelter! Mutual fear during wartime brought out great kindness among people, an attribute that could well be extended to peacetime.

My family's experience of the Second World War was minimal; their produce was vital to the war effort and also supplemented the rations they received. The little village of Ibstone in the Chiltern Hills was a comparative oasis of tranquility, as was Turville, down the hill from the Manor Farm where Monty's family lived. They were given the rental of this farm when the previous tenant had been dismissed as it was discovered that he was *"up to his eyes in the black market!"* Monty was a fully committed member of the Home Guard so brilliantly depicted in the TV series, 'Dad's Army.' It had all the trappings of the old established order with the Lord of the Manor in charge but which would never be the same again after the war.

As the enormity of war began to dawn upon me, I realized the extent to which we had escaped its full horrors and it was only after the war that my pacifist feelings began to take shape. It was the fear of the bomb – and we walked under the banner of the CND and peace education. As a mother of two young daughters, I felt the overwhelming need to protect them and have concentrated on peaceful solutions in my work and books on education. Today as an active Quaker, combined with Buddhism, I still put my energies into promoting the teaching of Peaceful Conflict Resolution and live in hope that these ideas will gain a wider foothold within the education system.

Biography

Mildred Masheder, *née Clinkard,* was born in the Oxfordshire village of Elsfield in August 1917, a farmer's daughter, a life she recounts in her auto-biography of her village childhood, *Carrier's Cart to Oxford.* Mildred studied Modern Languages at Oxford University, from 1939-42, as she describes in *From the Shires to the Spires,* and she has a Diploma in Education from London University.

After twenty years working as a primary teacher, Mildred became a senior lecturer in child development and multicultural studies at the University of North London.

Mildred's books on education include: *Recapturing Childhood, Let's Cooperate, Let's Enjoy Nature, Freedom from Bullying, Windows to Nature, Positive Childhood,* and the play section of *Natural Childhood.* She has also produced a video on cooperative play and parachute games.

Mildred has two children and two grandchildren and lives in North London. She is a practising Quaker, and an active member of *Growing Old Disgracefully.* She also paints and makes ceramics and is an avid theatre and opera-goer. At present, in her 94th year, she is doing research for a video-documentary on positive attitudes to growing old.